LEGENDS OF WARFARE

GROUND

M2/M3 Bradley

America's Cavalry/Infantry Fighting Vehicle

CHRISTIAN M. DEJOHN

Schiffer Publishing Ltd.

4880 Lower Valley Road • Atglen, PA 19310

Other Schiffer Books by the Author:
For Want of a Gun: The Sherman Tank Scandal of WWII
  (978-0-7643-5250-8)
M1 Abrams: America's Main Battle Tank (978-0-7643-5452-6)

Other Schiffer Books on Related Subjects:
*Duty Before Self: The Story of the 781st Tank Battalion
  in World War II* by John T. Mitzel (978-0-7643-4340-7)
Operation Dragoon: Autopsy of a Battle
  by Jean-Loup Gassend (978-0-7643-4580-7)
G-2: Intelligence for Patton by Brig. Gen. Oscar W. Koch
  (978-0-7643-0800-0)

Designed by Justin Watkinson
Type set in Impact/Minion Pro/Univers LT Std

ISBN: 978-0-7643-5588-2
Printed in China

Published by Schiffer Publishing, Ltd.
4880 Lower Valley Road
Atglen, PA 19310
Phone: (610) 593-1777; Fax: (610) 593-2002
E-mail: Info@schifferbooks.com
www.schifferbooks.com

For our complete selection of fine books on this and related
subjects, please visit our website at www.schifferbooks.com.
You may also write for a free catalog.

Schiffer Publishing's titles are available at special discounts for
bulk purchases for sales promotions or premiums. Special editions,
including personalized covers, corporate imprints, and excerpts
can be created in large quantities for special needs. For more
information, contact the publisher.

We are always looking for people to write books on new
and related subjects. If you have an idea for a book,
please contact us at proposals@schifferbooks.com.

Acknowledgments

As with my *For Want of a Gun: The Sherman Tank Scandal of World War II* and *M1 Abrams* books, a heroic squad of friends, family, supporters, and fellow United States Army veterans stepped up to help me cross the finish line with this book. Retired US Army Command Sgt. Maj. Rick Young, Executive Director of the National Armor and Cavalry Heritage Foundation, enabled me to wander through a motor pool of captured Soviet AFVs, IFVs, and tanks at Ft. Benning, Georgia, a walk that drove home to me how much our Cold War rivals spurred the success of the Bradley. Retired US Marine Maj. Len Dyer, Director of the US Army Armor and Cavalry Training Support Facility at Ft. Benning, while a "Devil Dog," does a great job taking care of the Army's tanks and passing on a proud heritage to new soldiers and Marines. Please visit www.armorcavalryheritagefoundation.org and help build a world-class tank museum at Ft. Benning to honor America's armor and cavalry heritage.

At Ft. Benning's National Infantry Museum, Director of Communications Cyndy Cerbin and Museum Director Frank Hanner helped me tell the story of "Bravo 1-4," a Bradley that now holds a place of honor in this impressive museum.

LTC Steve Russell, US Army (Ret.), author of *We Got Him! A Memoir of the Hunt and Capture of Saddam Hussein*, and now a congressman from Oklahoma's 5th District, honored me by contributing his personal insight on "Bravo 1-4." Though I'm an old cavalryman, I would have loved to serve with him in his 1-22 Infantry, the "Regulars."

Fellow Bosnia veteran SFC David Neuzil, project officer in the Army's Office of the Chief of Armor, lent his decades of hands-on Bradley experience to steer me in the right direction, to help an old tanker get the Bradley right. Other Army veterans that gave unstinting support and encouragement include Vietnam War heroes BG Bill Matz, AUS (Ret.), now serving as the secretary of the American Battle Monuments Commission, and Col. (Commendatore) Ralph Riccio. At the US Army Military History Institute at Carlisle Barracks, Pennsylvania, Tom Buffenbarger again came through with outstanding and courteous research support in making a rare, early Bradley "A-Zero" CFV accessible for research and photos, and clarifying its history.

Contents

Steady support and encouragement came from old friends and best men/groomsmen like Ed McGrath, Sam Hillanbrand, Christopher Freind, Adam Foxx, Cmdr. Steve Morgan, USN, and two of my old 1/104th Cavalry tank platoon sergeants, SFC Logan Fenstermacher and SFC Christopher Heyman, who, while we were serving in places as varied as the ice and snow of Ft. Drum, New York, to the swamps of Ft. Stewart, Georgia, to the Sahara Desert near Alexandria, Egypt—not to mention our deployment to Bosnia-Herzegovina in 2002–2003—never failed to yell down at me in my M1A1 Abrams Gunner's station, "Hey DeJohn, you need to write books about this Army stuff!"

At Schiffer Books, Bob Biondi proves once again the advantages of editing in a Hawaiian shirt with cigar blazing. Carey Massimini helped me knock out some great photos.

Closest to home, my wife, Lindsay—as with my other books—was always there to motivate, inspire, and support me. She cheerfully shared our honeymoon in Ireland with vintage tanks, flying boats, fortresses, warplanes, and the inspiring spirit of Gen. Michael Collins—a perennial good sport!

Foreword by Rep. Steve Russell

When the Bradley Fighting Vehicle was first fielded, critics complained that it couldn't do a myriad of tasks to support the infantry: It couldn't swim. It couldn't hold a full squad of riflemen. It couldn't fight tanks effectively. Its gun was too big—or too small—or too heavy for soldiers to manipulate. Its armor wasn't thick enough.

Through the lens of history, the Bradley Fighting Vehicle has not only proven to be successful and ubiquitous, but the soldiers operating it have found ways to maximize its potential and even perform tasks that it was never intended to do. Such is the case with many of history's successful weapon systems.

For all of the criticism, infantrymen have been able to maneuver Bradleys in almost any environment, from the rolling farmlands of Europe to deserts, to difficult, hilly or broken terrain, to tight, rough urban environments. The soldiers disgorged from the Bradley's hull are able to provide reconnaissance, secure key terrain, or fight through stubborn enemies with a variety of weapons at their disposal. Compared to its predecessor, the M113 Armored Personnel Carrier, the M2/M3 has not only exceeded every task of the M113, it performed many others beyond it.

In 1999, I learned this firsthand while conducting Bradley combat operations in the initial entry forces into Kosovo, in mountainous surroundings with rich farmland between key urban areas. The M2/M3's versatility was driven home with even greater intensity in Iraq, where I commanded the Bradley-equipped 1-22 Infantry task force. We operated in a combination of environments in the urban city of Tikrit, in the lush Tigris River valley, abutted by empty deserts. The M2/M3, I found, gave my infantry mobility, support and lethality that never failed us in the complex, adjoining terrain.

The Bradley wasn't invulnerable. In the Balkans, we repaired damage to them from minor anti-personnel mine strikes. The M2/M3 protected our soldiers from small arms and mortar fragmentation, and on multiple occasions in Kosovo, saved soldiers' lives. In Iraq, the weaponry used against us was more diverse, and we suffered losses of both vehicles and equipment. I lost several Bradleys and soldiers to anti-tank mines and RPGs.

Still, many other strikes—both improvised and conventional— were warded off, and the Bradley's accurate, lethal weapons systems allowed us to quickly dominate any firefight. Our optics and thermals enabled us to see enemies that couldn't see us. The ability to evacuate our wounded while protected against small arms fire allowed for life-saving transport to other locations. Despite its early critics, the Bradley never failed us, or our mission.

Today, one fine surviving example of a Bradley used in battle is located at Ft. Benning, Georgia, in the US Army's National Infantry Museum. As visitors trek up the Infantry Walk covering wars from the Revolution to Iraq, they encounter "Bravo 1-4," a Bradley from Task Force 1-22 Infantry that was used in the hunt for Saddam Hussein. This particular Bradley brings out great emotion in me; several of my soldiers were wounded in it and the driver, Specialist James E. Powell, was killed in action in this very vehicle. Through great persistence, I was able to secure "Bravo 1-4" for the museum from the bone yard at Texas' Red River Army Depot. While the vehicle appears intact, underneath it is a cover placed over a table-sized hole created by an anti-tank mine. Food Machinery Corporation (FMC), the M2/M3's designer and builder, graciously restored the cosmetic appearance of the vehicle along with the fine folks at the National Infantry Museum. Today it serves as a tribute to these soldiers, and to all those who have fought in Bradley Cavalry and Infantry Fighting Vehicles.

Just as Sherman tanks and White half-tracks made their mark on US military historical images in World War II, the Bradley Fighting Vehicle and the M1 Abrams tank will be the dominant historical images of combat operations from the Gulf War to the Balkans to operations in Iraq.

It is an honor for me to write the foreword to fellow US Army Balkans veteran Christian DeJohn's book, which is both an addition to the Bradley's historical record, and a tribute to those who have soldiered in it to defend the United States' interests around the globe.

Steve Russell
US Congressman
Lieutenant Colonel, US Army (*Ret.*)
Author, *We Got Him! A Memoir of the Hunt and Capture of Saddam Hussein*

An Oklahoma native, Steve Russell served twenty-one years as a US Army Infantry officer in Kosovo, Kuwait, Afghanistan, and Iraq. In 2003–04, he commanded Task Force 1-22 Infantry, 4th Infantry Division, which played a central part in the capture of Saddam Hussein. His decorations include the Legion of Merit, the Bronze Star Medal with Valor Device and Oak Leaf Cluster, and the Combat Infantryman's Badge. Upon retiring from the US Army in 2006, Russell created "Vets for Victory," touring the country as a motivational speaker. He also founded Two Rivers Arms, a small business that makes copies of Iraq's Tabuk AK-47 rifle. He was elected to the US House of Representatives in 2014, representing Oklahoma's Fifth District. His assignments include the House Armed Services Committee and House Committee on Government Oversight and Reform.

Foreword by SFC David Neuzil

The M2/M3 Bradley is both loved and hated by its crewmen, because the "Brad" has gone through many trials and tribulations to get to this point. I had the pleasure of serving on M3A1, M3A2, and M3A3 Cavalry Fighting Vehicles (CFVs). In 1996, as a new, young Bradley driver, I was sent to Bosnia in the first group of replacements sent to support the 1st Armored Division's mission. As part of IFOR's Operation Joint Endeavor, my C Troop, 1-1 CAV used M3A2s. Comanche Troop also returned to Bosnia in 1998 for Operations Joint Guard and Joint Forge, equipped with M2A2 Infantry Fighting Vehicles (IFVs). As a thirty-two-ton armored vehicle, the Bradley was well suited to traversing the bombed-out roads and small bridges that littered the landscape of war-torn Bosnia-Herzegovina, and we completed hundreds of patrols and checkpoints during this first deployment.

In summer 1996, the 1-1 CAV shot gunnery at Taborflava, southeast of Budapest. This was one of several bases the Hungarian Army allowed us to set up to move troops in and out of the Balkan theater. We used Bradleys provided by US Army Europe, both M3A2 CFVs and M2A2 IFVs.

Qualifying on Bradley gunnery in Hungary was interesting because the range had been set up for Soviet-style, Warsaw Pact vehicles. As a Bradley driver on his first time shooting gunnery, I was concerned about executing proper berm drills and keeping a steady platform for on-the-move engagements. Fortunately, being on the Platoon Leader's Bradley, I had an experienced gunner; this was his sixth or seventh time. He had served on a Bradley in Desert Storm, and loved it. My platoon alone had three Bradley Master Gunners in it, and training on the M2/M3 was paramount to them. We fired all of the gunnery tables, from an individual Bradley to Section level gunnery (three Bradleys firing at the same time). The troopers I served with in 1-1 CAV had confidence in their Bradleys and, more importantly, were proficient with them.

In 2006, I was a Scout Platoon Sergeant assigned to K Troop, 3/3 Armored Cavalry Regiment (3rd ACR), Ft. Hood, Texas. After receiving the latest version of the M3A3 CFV, my platoon spent a few months on new equipment training (NET), to bring us up to speed on the -A3's new fire control and digital systems. I was immediately impressed with the Bradley's upgrades. I especially liked the Commander's Independent Viewer (CIV), which allowed me to view the battlefield independently of the hull or turret's orientation. It was equipped with both a daytime television sight and a second generation, thermal viewer night sight. Their magnification allowed me to select targets for my gunner and put him on the target I was viewing in milliseconds.

In late 2007, the 3rd ACR deployed to Northern Iraq for fifteen months, in support of the 25th Infantry Division. My Cavalry Squadron, assigned to the city of Mosul, brought six Bradleys from Ft. Hood. My troop operated on both sides of the Tigris River; most of the heavy fighting was on the west side of the river, in the Al Jadidah and Az Zanjili neighborhoods. Often we'd patrol with two Bradleys and four HMMWVs—the Bradleys continuously patrolled the main streets, while the smaller Humvees were able to get down narrower streets. We had two incidents where Bradleys ran over pressure-plate activated Improvised Explosive Devices. One vehicle lost a track; the other one, hitting a larger IED, lost a track and a road wheel. Both Bradleys were quickly repaired and put back into action in a short time. Their crews, it should be noted, were unharmed.

My Platoon Leader and I had planned to use our two-Bradley section for mounted reconnaissance, rolling support by fire, and as armored casualty evacuation vehicles. The last role was put to the test on November 12, 2008, when an Iraqi Army soldier turned on my men and opened fire in a courtyard. One of my soldiers was killed instantly, and six more lay wounded. Using mostly Bradleys, we were able to save all but one of the soldiers we evacuated to the Combat Support Hospital in Mosul. One man had been mortally wounded, but made it to the hospital before succumbing to his wounds. For all the casualties we took in Iraq, none that I'm aware of were on the M2/M3, and if we hadn't had those two Bradleys in a patrol mode around us, we would never have been able to evacuate that many casualties so effectively.

Anyone can find fault with an armored vehicle—especially one with a "checkered" past like the M2/M3—but I found the Bradleys I served on to be solid performers. I really learned what the Bradley was capable of; if it broke down, it was because you weren't keeping up with maintenance, not because the M2/M3 was mechanically flawed. The same held true for the 25 mm Bushmaster main gun. In all my time, I never saw a main gun malfunction that wasn't the fault of the crew.

If you ask me, the strength of a vehicle lies in the crew's understanding of it. I knew what my Bradley's strengths and weaknesses were, and tried to exploit the strengths while avoiding the weaknesses.

David Neuzil,
Sergeant First Class, US Army (Ret.), MBA
Armor Project Officer, Office of the Chief of Armor, USA Armor School
Ft. Benning, Georgia

David Neuzil is an M2/M3 Bradley Armor Project Officer in the US Army's Office of the Chief Of Armor, United States Armor School, Ft. Benning, Georgia. His experience with the M2/M3 Bradley includes the M3A1, M3A2, and M3A3 variants. His awards include the Bronze Star Medal with Valor Device, Purple Heart, Army Commendation Medal, Iraq Campaign Medal with three Bronze service stars, the Order of Saint George, Silver and Bronze Medallions, and Combat Spurs.

Introduction

To those who came of age after the Cold War, the M2 Bradley Infantry Fighting Vehicle (IFV) and M3 Cavalry Fighting Vehicle (CFV) have been an integral part of the US Army's inventory for decades. While not as imposing as its muscular bigger brother, the M1 Abrams tank, the Bradley has compiled a solid record from the Gulf War of 1991, to places like Somalia, Bosnia, Kosovo, Afghanistan, and Iraq.

But younger readers may not be aware that the Bradley was the subject of a firestorm of debate from the 1970s into the 1990s, opposed by President Jimmy Carter and damned in newspaper and magazine articles. It was even the subject of a black comedy film implying that Army NCOs and officers were bribed by the defense industry to hide the Bradley's flaws and fake test results; to (as the old Army saying goes) "put a ribbon on a turd." The Bradley—angry critics assured us—was a lemon, a flammable, under-armored death trap.

This criticism was largely politically motivated, from journalists who longed for the Vietnam era, where the most far-fetched accusations against the US military were unquestioningly accepted and splashed across front pages. Pundits also sought a way to attack President Ronald Reagan and his popular rebuild of the American military, badly depleted and demoralized after Vietnam.

Much of the furor derived from media ignorance of basic Army doctrine and equipment. Media critics confused the Bradley with a tank, comparing it unfavorably to the M1 Abrams while lamenting, "Why can't it have as much armor/firepower as a tank?"

The Bradley was designed for a specific role, distinct from a Main Battle Tank (MBT): more than just a "battle taxi" to transport men to and from battle in safety, it would allow them to fight from inside it, with a fair chance to engage and destroy the enemy in lightly armored, Soviet-built vehicles. It was also designed to work in conjunction with other weapons, forming a triumvirate that became symbols of the Reagan era's proud, resurgent US Army: the Bradley, the M1 Abrams tank, and the AH-64 Apache helicopter gunship.

While Apaches scanned the route ahead of American ground forces, looking for enemy armor, and the Abrams was designed to fight the enemy's best tanks, the M3 CFV would fulfill traditional scouting and reconnaissance roles of the US Cavalry, while the M2 IFV would provide infantry support as needed. The TOW missile and 25 mm Bushmaster gave the Bradley an impressive leg up in comparison to its M113 predecessor, but—the critics notwithstanding—it was never intended to equal or surpass the Abrams' lethal ability and armor protection.

Angry pundits focusing on the Bradley's relatively thin armor and 25 mm Bushmaster cannon made unfair comparisons to the Abrams tank. They seemed willfully unaware that the Bradley's main job wasn't to duel head-to-head with powerful Soviet tanks, though it had a fighting chance to immobilize or destroy them.

In the Gulf War of 1991, approximately twenty Bradleys were destroyed in "Blue-On-Blue" or "Friendly Fire" accidents: in the confusing heat of battle at places like Medina Ridge and 73 Easting, Iraqi tanks and soft-skinned vehicles were mixed in with American Bradleys, not a good situation for young, eager tank gunners. These tragedies seemed to "confirm" media criticism that the Bradley—having been destroyed by American tanks—was not as good as a tank.

These accidents led to improvements in both US Army doctrine and equipment; American tanks and IFVs and CFVs now carry high-tech gadgets to sort out who is who on the battlefield, and to reduce confusion during the "fog of war." Army doctrine and SOP also includes procedures for a commander to quickly identify his vehicles, and to verify identity before giving his gunner the order to fire.

The Bradley went on to overcome the politically motivated criticism, giving good service in later wars in Afghanistan and Iraq. During these conflicts, the M2/M3 was updated with crew-served weapons stations, further armor and ballistic glass protection, reactive armor tiles and boxes, communications gear, etc., all of which showed the basic adaptability and utility of the decades-old design. A vehicle intended to supplement the 1960s-era M113 Armored Personnel Carrier of Vietnam fame replaced it, and will likely continue in Army service for decades.

As a cavalry tank gunner myself, in an M1A1 Abrams, I knew that we tankers would work closely with Bradleys in a full-blown deployment. While training at places like Ft. Stewart, Georgia;Ft. Drum, New York; Ft. Knox, Kentucky; and Hohenfels, Germany, I often saw Bradleys and their crews nearby; we all ate the same dust. I recall meeting groups of proud Bradley crewmen training near my 1/104th Cavalry at Ft. Stewart around the year 2000, and learning they were preparing to deploy to a Godforsaken place known as Bosnia–Herzegovina. "Those poor bastards," many of us 1/104th CAV troopers empathized.

Ironically enough, the 1/104th Cavalry would be deployed to the same country soon after the September 11, 2001 attacks, essentially as MOS 19 Deltas (dismounted Cavalry Scouts)—although, in spite of a year of active duty that encompassed months of training in the role, and seven months of actually doing it, we were never formally awarded the title. And we rolled in up-armored Humvees, not Bradleys.

Although an old Abrams tanker, my appreciation for the Bradley has a personal dimension to it. In Bosnia, my Apache Troop (Forward)'s assigned "Area of Responsibility" (AOR) in NATO's Multinational Division North was Brcko, where Bradleys had been used to help quell the notorious "Brcko Riots" of 1997. And in the confusing post-September 11 reorganization of many Army units, at one point, my 1/104th Cavalry was scheduled to turn in its Abrams tanks for Bradleys.

Decades after the critics have been silenced, this unglamorous but reliable, adaptable vehicle soldiers on, well into a new century. Like its namesake, General Omar Bradley of World War II fame, the M2/M3 may be overshadowed by others who are louder, more glamorous and photogenic, but to the thousands of American GIs who have grown to appreciate them in far-flung conflicts, its record of dependable, down-to-earth service stands and continues.

CHAPTER 1
Design, Construction, and Background

Courtesy of *The Commercial Vehicle*

"THE BEST TRUCK EVER MADE"

One of the types of Liberty trucks which are being used by the American forces. Every one of its parts has been standardized, and it is the product of the combined genius of the motor truck industry and the War Department

The first US troop transports were unarmed, and similar to commercial trucks for civilian use. *Photo courtesy US Army Transportation Museum*

The year 2017 was the centenary of American entry into World War I. Back then, tales abounded of Paris being saved in 1914, when French troops were rushed to the Marne front in commandeered civilian taxis. Once the Yanks went "Over There," the US Army soon adopted commercial trucks for troop transportation.

As noted in *For Want Of A Gun: The Sherman Tank Scandal of World War II*, when the revolutionary tank debuted in the Great War, often armies were unable to exploit breakthroughs by moving supporting infantry up to take advantage of penetrations and to pursue fleeing enemies.

It's not too far-fetched to imagine a 1918 doughboy rolling "Up the Argonne" in an Army truck and daydreaming, "If we added some salvaged Hun armor plate to the sides of this thing, it would give some protection to the doughs riding in it." As for firepower, "Why not add some borrowed Chauchats (French light machine guns) to the cabin; then we could fire out, while on the move."

In the decades after the 1918 Armistice, Germany pioneered troop transports to accompany its tanks, but the US Army was doing it, too. Open-topped, lightly armored, and armed half-tracks in which GIs would ride, then dismount and fight on foot were not the last word in what would come to be called "infantry fighting vehicles" (IFVs), but they were certainly an advance over the humble, canvas-topped "Liberty Trucks" of 1918.

Before the Second World War ended, the US Army was planning the next generation of troop transport, with decent armor and weapons, in which the troops inside would be more than passengers.

This led to a bevy of limited production vehicles often too big, too heavy, and not amphibious. But the seeds had been planted, and eventually American soldiers got the M113, one of the best Armored Personnel Carriers (APCs) of the postwar era.

By the 1960s, when the Soviet Union had introduced fast, lightly armed, and armored IFVs such as the BMP-1, the US was falling behind. It's hard for younger readers to appreciate today, but the eventual success of the M2/M3 Bradley was spurred on by Soviet advances. As Gen. William DePuy told Congress in 1977: "Almost every army you look at is ahead of the American Army, as far as taking care of our infantry. The Russians are ahead of us, the Germans are ahead of us, the Dutch are ahead of us, the French are ahead of us, the Yugoslavians are ahead of us. Almost everybody has a better infantry vehicle than the US Army."

It may surprise younger viewers, but in the fervent anti-military climate of the post-Vietnam War US, the Bradley became a lightning rod for fierce debate. "The history of the Bradley," wrote retired Gen. Stan Sheridan (the Army's first Bradley Program Manager), "was long and tortured." It was damned in print as "The Army's $13 Billion Death Trap," an alleged fraud and waste of taxpayer money; even the subject of a satirical movie over what a failure—the armchair quarterbacks assured us—it would surely be in future combat. But after President Ronald Reagan restored funds cancelled by the Carter administration, the Bradley, with its big brother M1 Abrams tank, came to embody the rebuilt, resurgent, confident, Reagan-era US Army.

But it wasn't smooth riding just yet—after Bradleys were tragically lost to friendly fire in the Persian Gulf War of 1991, the

American soldiers going into action "up in the Argonne" in Fall 1918, rode in trucks like this "Standard B" Liberty, whose builders included Diamond T, Packard, and Pierce-Arrow. While grateful for the step up from marching or riding horse-drawn carriages, one imagines that the doughboys rued the lack of armor protection and defensive and offensive weapons on the Army's first "battle taxis." Some 7,000 of these trucks went "Over There." *Photo courtesy US Army Transportation Museum*

While the German Army gets much credit for mobilizing some of its infantry, the US Army was developing the concept as well: an M3 half-track at Ft. Knox, Kentucky, June 1942. While the open top and thin armor were problematic, it was a great advance over transporting troops in unarmed, unarmored trucks, as was the norm in the Great War. *Photo courtesy US Army Military History Institute*

To these GIs in training at Ft. Knox, in June 1942, the Bradley's troop compartment might not seem entirely unfamiliar—the back of the M3 was also cramped. Halftracks were better than trucks, but there was room for improvement, especially in crew protection. Eventually, US wartime armor divisions would include three battalions of armored infantry riding in halftracks like the M3. *Photo courtesy US Army Military History Institute*

media attacks resumed. The Army responded by incorporating some of the latest advances in communication and methods of IFF (Identification of Friend and Foe) into subsequent variants, technology that, while taken for granted today, was revolutionary in the early 1990s, like digital communication between vehicles and onboard Global Positioning Systems (GPS) linked to satellites.

In the Afghanistan and Iraq Wars since 2001 and 2003, Bradley crews have faced new generations of more powerful antitank weapons, mines, IEDs, booby traps, etc. Luckily, the M2/M3's designers back in the 1960s and 1970s anticipated this, providing for bolt-on layers of increased armor protection. Already an ugly duckling covered with nuts and bolts, the Bradley took on an even more pronounced Frankenstein-like appearance, piling on reactive armor boxes and tiles, spaced armor, more crew weapons stations, more antennas, etc. Compared to today's Rube Goldberg clunkers, the relatively sleek M3 Bradley CFV of 1983 looks like a veritable cigarette boat by comparison.

But Bradley crews aren't complaining; while the domineering, more glamorous M1 Abrams tank often hogs the spotlight and the glory, the low-key but dependable Bradley has rolled on, now approaching its fourth decade of faithful service. The much-maligned "death trap" of the late 1970s and early 1980s—the subject of fierce political debates in presidential campaigns—has matured to become one of the best infantry and cavalry fighting vehicles in the world.

This chapter features a brief photo survey of some of the designs that led to today's M2 IFV/M3 CFV.

GIs ham it up during the Army's epic 1941 Louisiana Maneuvers. Half-tracks like this used a rear door for troops to quickly mount and dismount, not unlike the one on the Bradley that would appear decades later. *Photo courtesy US Army Military History Institute*

Shortly before Pearl Harbor, Tommy gun-equipped troops of the author's 1/104th Cavalry clown for the camera in a half-track armed with two water-cooled Browning .30 caliber machine guns. Note that like the present-day Bradley, the side of the vehicle is crowded with soldiers' gear strapped to the sides. *Photo courtesy author's collection*

One of the first US postwar Armored Personnel Carriers (APCs), the open-topped M39 was derived from the wartime M18 Hellcat tank destroyer. Here, Marines use it to evacuate casualties during the fighting for Boulder City in Korea, 1953. *US Army photo by Sgt. Cholakis*

In Cold War Germany, 1954, open-topped, thinly armored World War II–era half-tracks are replaced by the newer M75 APC, whose production was halted that year in favor of the new M59 design. *Photo courtesy US Army Military History Institute*

First built in 1945, the M44 Armored Personnel Carrier began to replace wartime half-tracks around 1948. It carried a crew of three and up to twenty-four GIs in a rear compartment. The armored personnel carrier concept, to carry soldiers into battle in safety and to keep up with tanks, was coming along, but the M44 was too large and heavy, at 51,000 pounds. *Photo courtesy US Army Military History Institute*

The M75 armored infantry vehicle saw limited service in the Korean War. Some 1,780 were built. It was almost ten feet tall, not amphibious, and vulnerable to enemy fire through its engine grills. But its manufacturer, FMC, gained experience that was applied to the future M113 APC. *Photo courtesy US Army Military History Institute*

A restored M75 struts its stuff. Notice the resemblance to the soon-to-come M113. *Photo courtesy Wormwood The Star*

1959: 16th Infantry Regiment, First Infantry Division soldiers load up into an M59 APC for a training exercise in Germany. *Photo courtesy US Army Military History Institute*

GIs of the 51st Infantry Regiment, 4th Armored Division train with M59 APCs in Ulm, Germany, in the 1950s. The M59's influence on the M113 that followed it can be seen in the use of a ramp and folding seats in a rear troop compartment. *Photo courtesy US Army Military History Institute*

An M113 Armored Cavalry Assault Vehicle (ACAV) of the 1/1 Cavalry, attached to the 23rd ("Americal") Division. The ACAV featured gun turrets and improved armor over the standard M113. *Photo courtesy US Army Military History Institute*

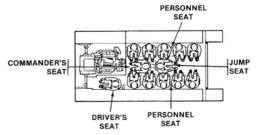

The Bradley's seating arrangements owe much to the M113's, seen here. *Courtesy US Army Technical Manual TM 9-2350-277-10*

West Berlin, 1961. GIs at Checkpoint Charlie confront the Red Army with an M59 APC and M48 Patton tank. *Photo courtesy US Army Military History Institute*

Vietnam, 1967. Overhead view of an M113 ACAV of the 11th Armored Cavalry Regiment ("The Black Horse.) The large troop hatch in the rear would be retained in the Bradley's design. *Photo courtesy US Army Military History Institute*

Notice the trim vane, the flat, rectangular engine access cover on the front of this M113 ACAV from the 17th Cavalry in Vietnam, 1968. Like the large crew hatch on the top rear, this feature would be carried over to the M2/M3 Bradley. *Photo courtesy US Army Military History Institute*

The ACAV increased the firepower and crew protection of American AFVs. The motto stenciled onto a gun turret hatch of this one in Vietnam, 1968 (attached to the 11th Armored Cavalry Regiment), embodies the aggressive Cavalry spirit. *Photo courtesy US Army Military History Institute*

This front view of a 3/5 Cavalry ("The Black Knights") ACAV, attached to the 9th Infantry Division in Vietnam, shows the front gun turret and extra armor kit, added both in the field and eventually at the factory. Decades later, Bradley crewmen in Afghanistan and Iraq would receive modifications such as the Bradley Urban Survivability Kit (BUSK) for their mounts. *Photo courtesy US Army Military History Institute*

The Soviet BTR series of armored personnel carriers is a typical opponent of the Bradley. Shown at the May 2011 victory parade in Moscow to commemorate the end of World War II, this BTR-80 variant was introduced in 1986, an improvement on the prior BTR-60 and BTR-70. *Photo courtesy Vitaly Kuzmin*

The Red Army pioneered an effective infantry fighting vehicle (IFV) in the mid-1960s, the BMP-1. The Bradley's primary opponent was to be light Soviet armor (such as this captured Iraqi BMP at Ft. Benning), while head-on duels with Soviet tanks would be left to its big brother, the M1 Abrams Main Battle Tank (MBT). But in its early years, the M2/M3 was damned by media critics who misunderstand the battlefield role and capabilities of an IFV versus an MBT. *Photo courtesy National Armor and Cavalry Heritage Foundation*

THE BMP, CAPTURED DURING COMBAT
OPERATIONS IN THE EUPHRATES RIVER
VALLEY OF IRAQ (OPERATION DESERT
STORM), IS PRESENTED TO THE UNITED
STATES ARMY ARMOR CENTER BY THE
SOLDIERS OF THE 24TH INFANTRY
DIVISION (MECHANIZED).

7 MAY 1991

A plaque on an Iraqi BMP (captured in 1991, by Desert Storm GIs of the 24th Infantry Division), discovered by the author in a Ft. Benning motor pool. Equipped throughout its history with handheld anti-tank weapons such as the M-72A2 LAW, AT-4, M47 Dragon, and FGM-148 Javelin, the M2/M3 allows Infantry soldiers to destroy enemy light armor and IFVs. Furthermore, the TOW missile gives them a fighting chance against the best Soviet-built tanks; while the first model TOWs could damage T-55s and T-62s, improved versions of the TOW can take out the T-64 and T-72. *Photo courtesy National Armor and Cavalry Heritage Foundation*

As the original caption states, Bradley crewmen use plastic scale models, "to train crews in target acquisition, range determination, and vehicle identification … the local Training Support Center can provide models in 1:10, 1:30, 1:35, and 1:60 scale." Among the friendly and enemy vehicles shown here are the M60, M113, BMP, BTR, ZSU-234, T-62, and T-72. *Illustration courtesy US Army FM 23-1, Bradley Gunnery*

Throughout the Cold War, the Soviet Union fielded a vast array of armor. While researching this book, the author found a PT-76 amphibious tank (left), one of the most common reconnaissance tanks of the Communist bloc, and the JS3 Stalin heavy tank (right), in a motor pool of captured Warsaw Pact equipment at Ft. Benning. While not as powerful as a tank, the Bradley was designed to give American infantrymen and cavalrymen enough firepower to defend against and defeat a wide variety of enemy armor. *Photo courtesy National Armor and Cavalry Heritage Foundation*

Another design on the road to the Bradley was the XM701 test bed vehicle, evolved from 1964's XM701 Mechanized Infantry Combat Vehicle (MICV-65). It featured sloped rear armor over a troop compartment, and firing ports for the crew to fight while moving. Although the design was cancelled due to reasons including poor automotive performance, its influence on the future M2/M3 design can be seen. *Photo courtesy US Army Military History Institute*

As well as the Soviet BMP series, the Bradley's design was influenced by the West German Marder AFV, first fielded in the early 1970s, and carrying a 20 mm cannon in a two-man turret. The US considered adopting the Marder, which features a troop compartment, decent anti-tank weapons, and the ability to keep up with main battle tanks. Here, a Marder M1A3 fires its MILAN wire-guided antitank missile at Grafenwoehr, in September 2004. *US Army photo by Paula Guzman*

The M113 APC was a versatile design that had served in a variety of roles for decades since the 1960s, but was outdated by the 1990s. Here, an M113 of the 7th Infantry Regiment, "The Cottonbalers," attached to the 24th Infantry Division, rolls on during the 1991 Persian Gulf War. A 1992 General Accounting Office report to Congress after Desert Storm found that most "113s" were unable to keep up with the Abrams tank and Bradley IFV/CFV. And as the Warsaw Pact introduced more powerful antitank weapons and better-armed IFVs, the US Army's need for a new generation IFV/CFV, faster and able to take on the latest Soviet bloc light armored vehicles, became obvious. *Photo Courtesy 7th Infantry Regiment Association*

Another influence on the Bradley was the Army's Armored Reconnaissance Scout Vehicle (ARSV) program; seen here is an XM800T prototype at Ft. Knox. Although the ARSV program was cancelled in 1974, the design influenced the later M2/M3, and the Food Machinery Corporation (FMC) applied some of the experience on this program to building the later M2/M3. *Photo courtesy TankNutDave.com*

In August 1968, Army Chief of Staff Gen. William Westmoreland brought together the Mechanized Infantry Combat Vehicle Ad Hoc Study Group (Casey Board), which ironed out problems with the XM723's development. In May 1977, the MICV concept evolved into the XM2 Infantry Fighting Vehicle (IFV) and XM3 Cavalry Fighting Vehicle (CFV). Here in December of that year, an XM723 is offloaded from a McDonnell Douglas YC-15 tactical transport during heavy loading tests. *US Army photo by Charles Connally*

A Bradley prototype on display at Camp Roberts, California. The XM2 (Infantry Fighting Vehicle) and XM3 (Cavalry Fighting vehicle) prototypes debuted in late 1978. After extensive evaluation, the Army adopted them as the M2 and M3 in late 1979, and the first production vehicles began to reach soldiers in the spring of 1981. According to a 1980 Congressional report, the "rollaway" cost of a fully equipped M2 or M3 was estimated at $557,000 each, in FY 1980 dollars. *Photo courtesy Frank Baldevarona*

The Army's MICV project of the 1960s led to the MIC-65 and later MICV-70, which evolved into the XM723. Researching this book at Ft. Benning, the author found this rare XM723 under a tarpaulin in a vast motor pool. This is one of twelve pilot vehicles built in 1972–73, and the direct predecessor of the M2/M3 Bradley. *Photo courtesy National Armor and Cavalry Heritage Foundation*

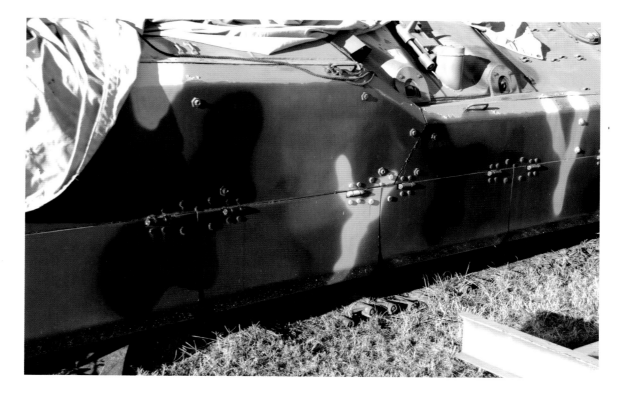

This front view of the XM723 shows its family resemblance to the eventual M2/M3. The XM723's one-man turret with a 20 mm cannon evolved into a two-man turret with the Bushmaster 25 mm cannon and TOW antitank missiles, all of which were incorporated into the final M2/M3 design. *Photo courtesy National Armor and Cavalry Heritage Foundation*

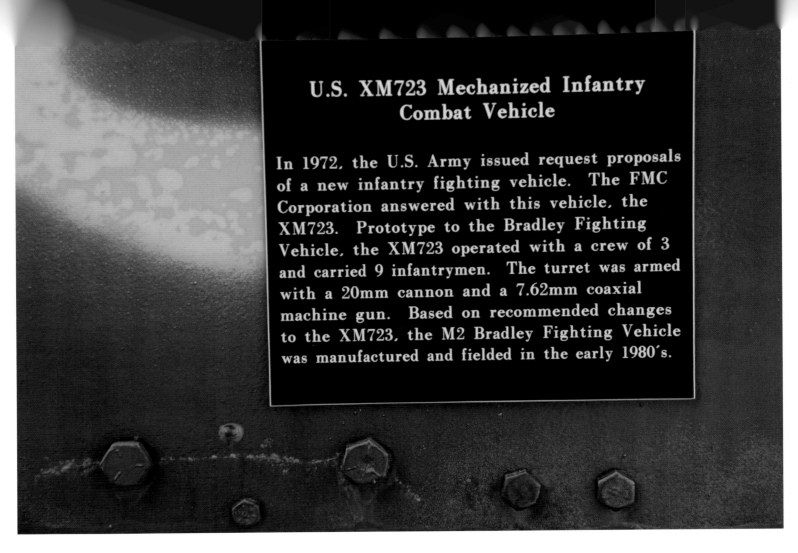

U.S. XM723 Mechanized Infantry Combat Vehicle

In 1972, the U.S. Army issued request proposals of a new infantry fighting vehicle. The FMC Corporation answered with this vehicle, the XM723. Prototype to the Bradley Fighting Vehicle, the XM723 operated with a crew of 3 and carried 9 infantrymen. The turret was armed with a 20mm cannon and a 7.62mm coaxial machine gun. Based on recommended changes to the XM723, the M2 Bradley Fighting Vehicle was manufactured and fielded in the early 1980's.

The data plate attached to the XM723 MICV pilot vehicle at Ft. Benning, which the author found under wraps in 2016. *Photo courtesy National Armor and Cavalry Heritage Foundation*

The XM723 was able to carry eleven soldiers. Here, an XM723 MICV pilot vehicle photographed at Ft. Benning in 2006, painted in a classic 1970s/early 1980s "MERDC" (Mobility Equipment Research and Development) paint scheme. Judging by the plaque on the right, this may be the same vehicle the author uncovered in 2016. *Photo by Craig Swain*

Right side firing ports on the XM723 MICV pilot vehicle at Ft. Benning. Rather than mere passengers riding passively in the rear of the vehicle, the initial Bradley design allowed troops to fight on the move from inside. *Photo by Craig Swain*

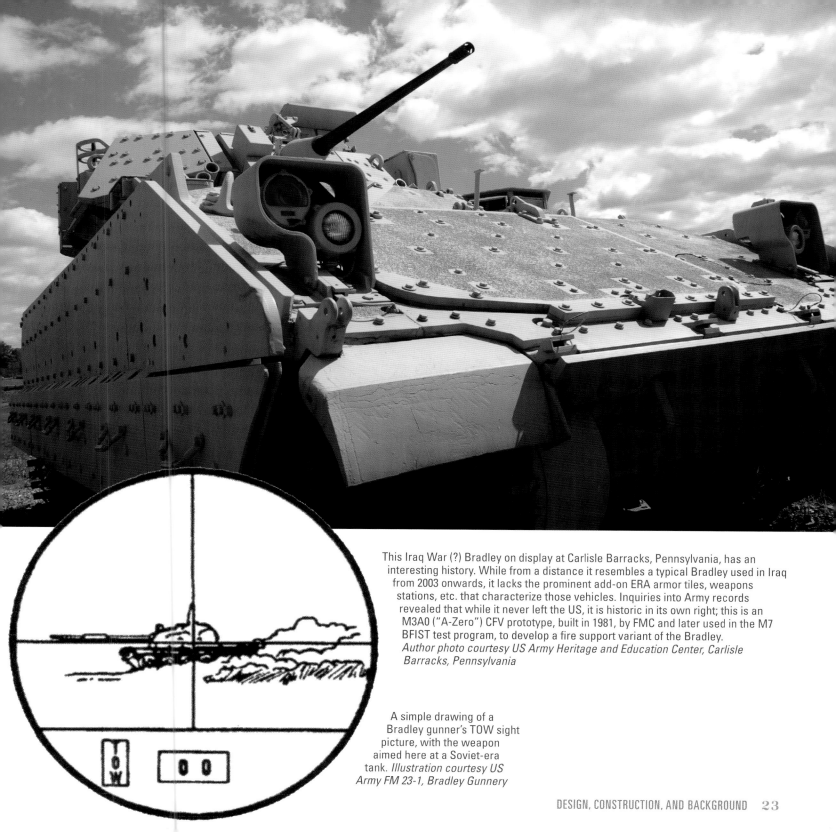

This Iraq War (?) Bradley on display at Carlisle Barracks, Pennsylvania, has an interesting history. While from a distance it resembles a typical Bradley used in Iraq from 2003 onwards, it lacks the prominent add-on ERA armor tiles, weapons stations, etc. that characterize those vehicles. Inquiries into Army records revealed that while it never left the US, it is historic in its own right; this is an M3A0 ("A-Zero") CFV prototype, built in 1981, by FMC and later used in the M7 BFIST test program, to develop a fire support variant of the Bradley. *Author photo courtesy US Army Heritage and Education Center, Carlisle Barracks, Pennsylvania*

A simple drawing of a Bradley gunner's TOW sight picture, with the weapon aimed here at a Soviet-era tank. *Illustration courtesy US Army FM 23-1, Bradley Gunnery*

An early M3 Bradley Cavalry Fighting Vehicle, built in 1982, and now on display at Ft. Benning. In 1976, the XM-723 MICV concept evolved into the XM2 Infantry Fighting Vehicle (IFV) and XM3 Cavalry Fighting Vehicle (CFV). After years of testing and further development, the first production M2s and M3s reached Army units in spring 1981. To the right is an M60 Patton tank, which soldiered on into the 1990s, until replaced by the M1 Abrams. *Author photo courtesy National Armor and Cavalry Heritage Foundation*

As detailed in the author's book on the M1 Abrams tank, the Bradley was intended to work closely with the new M1 tank. Gen. Stan Sheridan told Congress in February 1979, "there is an urgent requirement for Infantry and Cavalry fighting vehicles to fight side by side with the XM1 tank." The Bradley, he testified, "provides improved and versatile firepower; mobility compatible with the XM1; sufficiently increased protection to allow infantry and cavalry to fight from within the vehicle; and simplified maintenance." The Abrams-Bradley team became a visible symbol of President Reagan's rebuild of the US Army. These vehicles are painted in one of the classic early 1980s MERDC "Verdant" camouflage paint schemes. *US Army photo courtesy Department of Defense*

To the author, a teenager when the Bradley debuted in the 1980s, the M2/M3 still seems to be a "new" vehicle. FMC delivered ten prototype Bradleys for testing in December 1978, and the first production vehicle in May 1981. In this undated photo of GIs admiring a new Bradley, they wear post–Korean War–style "OG 107" fatigues and Vietnam-era baseball caps; note female soldier's 1970s style WAC (Women's Army Corps) skirt and cap. Since the Army's woodland camouflage Battle Dress Uniforms (BDUs) were not widely issued until October of 1981, it's likely that this photo precedes that date. *Photo courtesy author's collection*

At an October 20, 1981 dedication ceremony at Ft. Myer, Virginia, the M2 IFV was officially named after General of the Army Omar Nelson Bradley (1893–1981). Little known today is that it was originally planned to name the CFV version the "M3 Devers," after Bradley's peer Gen. Jacob Devers, but both the M2 and M3 variants have come to be known as "Bradleys."
Photo courtesy author's collection

Bookends. The many changes and additions to the Bradley through its decades of service can be dramatically seen by comparing an M3 CFV from the 1980s to an Iraq War M3A3 CFV with full reactive armor tiles and boxes.
1/35 scale models and photo by the author

CHAPTER 2
Operational Use

The first Bradleys began to reach Army units in 1983. Here, at a Ft. Benning, Georgia, live fire gunnery range in June of that year, M2 crewmen check their vehicle's 25 mm M242 Bushmaster "chain gun." The green range flag (right) indicates that they have yet to open fire.
US Army photo by SPC5 Bobby Mathis

This chapter is a visual survey of the Bradley's successful use around the world, as it approaches its fourth decade of service. While associated with the Iraq War lately, it's been used everywhere American infantry and cavalry have deployed, from Bosnia to South Korea to Poland.

As retired General Stan Sheridan has written, the Persian Gulf War of 1991, was a watershed in making and salvaging the Bradley's reputation: "The real proof of the Bradley was Desert Storm, where it received not only its baptism of fire in combat, but complete soldier acceptance. The experience of the lead brigade of the 24th Mechanized Infantry Division's "Left Hook" operation is typical ... the brigade's 120 Bradleys traveled 360 miles, fighting all the way, with no vehicle drop-outs or losses. While the 25 mm armor-piercing rounds did kill some T-72 tanks from the side and rear, it was an overkill against the Iraqis' infantry carriers. (Bradley rounds) passed right through the BMPs."

"The Bradley soldiers of Desert Storm and those using the vehicle in places like Somalia and Bosnia have resoundingly ... put to bed the nay-sayers, the questioners, and the critics by affirming that the Bradley is a highly mobile and effective battlefield killing machine ... justly touted as the finest fighting vehicle of its kind in the world."

As you view almost four decades of M2/M3 history, notice the variety of climates, paint schemes, and markings, and how, to meet the changing battlefield, the Bradley's appearance has been altered with more and more ugly but effective "bolt-on" armor and weapons packages.

June 1983. GIs at Ft. Benning use the swimming curtain on their M2—not unlike those used on the "DD" or "swimming" Sherman tanks of World War II—to cross a body of water, with the vehicle's turning tracks for propulsion. Top speed was four miles per hour. *US Army photo by SPC5 Bobby Mathis*

Senator Barry Goldwater checks out a M2 Bradley at the US Army Armor Center, then located at Ft. Knox, Kentucky, in January 1984. The vehicle is painted in one of the various MERDC camo schemes. *Photo by Chuck Croston, courtesy US National Archives*

Swimming Bradleys II. At Ft. Benning's Victory Pond, June 1983, M2s enter the water. While the early Bradleys had this amphibious capability, later, heavier variants (due to increased armor protection) prefer to use pontoon bridges to cross bodies of water. *US Army photo by SPC5 Bobby Mathis*

Operation Reforger, 1985. After decades of large US Army maneuvers, German civilians take this Bradley IFV of the 7th Infantry Regiment in stride. This M2 is participating in the "Central Guardian" phase of the wargame; note Hoffmann device clamped above the cannon to simulate fire. *US Army photo courtesy Department of Defense*

It's rare for soldiers to go to such lengths to camouflage their vehicles and persons, but these 41st Infantry, Second Armored Division GIs at Ft. Hood's Shell Point training area in January 1986, gave it their best. Foliage looks impressive on a parked vehicle or soldier standing at attention, but unless tightly secured, it can fall off a moving vehicle or man. From March 1985 – May 1987, the Army conducted live-fire tests to identify the Bradley's weak points. Many of these "survivability enhancements," such as a better Halon automatic fire extinguisher, relocated ammo storage, and modification of the internal fuel supply (all to reduce the risk of fire), added steel applique armor, spall liners, and attachment points for future use of reactive armor tiles, would be incorporated into the later M2A3/M3A3 variant. *Photo by William Rosenmund, courtesy US National Archives*

Close-up of Multiple Integrated Laser Engagement System (MILES) gear used to simulate 25 mm gunfire in training exercises, clamped to the barrel of an M2's main gun in 1986. Not seen is the rotating light used to indicate hits, which GIs call a "gumball machine" or "whoopee light." *Photo by William Rosenmund, courtesy US National Archives*

January, 1986. At Ft. Hood's Antelope Mound training area, soldiers of the 2nd Battalion, 41st Infantry Regiment, Second Armored Division—wearing classic 1980s Battle Dress Utilities (BDUs)—exit an M2's troop compartment. The thickness of the rear ramp's armor is evident. Notice the inward-slanting shape of the turret bustle rack, later enlarged to hold more gear. Orange light on right rear of turret is a MILES "whoopee light" to simulate hits. *Photo by William Rosenmund, courtesy US National Archives*

SHADOW HAWK, September 1987. During a phase of Exercise BRIGHT STAR '87, an M2A0 crew elevates their M242 Bushmaster cannon. Should the electronic gunsights in the turret fail, in front of the commander's hatch is a simple external sight, which enables him to quickly align the Bradley's turret with targets and "shoot from the hip," from zero to 360 mils. Note the Belgian M240 coaxial machine gun's "shroud" or cover, deleted from later models. Behind the headlights is the folding trim or bow vane, which facilitated amphibious operations. This M2 wears standard 1980s NATO 3-color camouflage, which replaced the solid green of the first M2s and M3s. *US Army photo courtesy Department of Defense*

SHADOW HAWK '87. An M2 opens fire with its M242 during BRIGHT STAR '87 multinational wargames. The light-colored tarp on the left rear of the vehicle highlights the storage racks for GI ammo cans. *US Army photo by PFC Prince Hearns*

September 1987. Although Desert Sand-painted Bradleys came to be associated with Desert Shield/ Desert Storm in 1990–91, the color had been used on US vehicles for years. Note the too-small turret bustle rack (later redesigned and enlarged) on this Bradley at the Port of Aquaba, Jordan, after Exercise SHADOW HAWK. *Photo by PH2 Elliot, USN courtesy National Archives*

November 1988. At the National Training Center (NTC), Ft. Irwin, California, a 24th Infantry (Mechanized) Division M2 sports a Desert Sand finish and black inverted "V" chevron formation/ tactical symbols, with the "V" representing the Division's "VICTORY" motto. The direction the "V" is pointing on a Bradley and smaller markings close to it (such as the two black squares seen here under the "V") indicate specific vehicles within a platoon. While these tactical markings became a common sight to the general public during the 1991 Persian Gulf War, this marking scheme had been in use since the 1980s. *US Army photo courtesy National Archives*

Right side view of another 24th Infantry (Mechanized) Division M2 at NTC, November 1988, crowded with the crew's gear on the turret and front slope. Rolls of barbed (concertina) wire are carried to set up hasty checkpoints and roadblocks, as the author learned when deployed to Bosnia in 2002–2003.
US Army photo courtesy National Archives

Fort Polk, Louisiana, April 1990. A new Bradley of the 3rd Squadron, 1st Cavalry Regiment—attached to the 5th Infantry Division (Mechanized)—is christened. The Chemical Agent Resistant Coating (CARC) paint used on the NATO 3-color scheme was designed to be smoother, easier to clean, and resistant to chemical agent contamination. Notice the inverted triangle shape of the rubber track blocks, in contrast to the later, rectangular "Big Foot" tracks. *US Army photo by Spec. Diana Lindsey courtesy National Archives*

Desert Shield, 1991. Some crews who deployed to the Persian Gulf War remembered the atypical camouflage schemes on Bradleys assigned to NTC in the late 1980s/early 1990s. Here, a 24th Infantry Division Bradley sports irregular broad gray stripes edged in black over the standard Desert Sand paint. These vehicles are likely engaged in gunnery training in Saudi Arabia before the ground campaign kicked off. Per range regulations, the closest Bradley displays a red warning flag to indicate firing, while the crew of the rear vehicle has elevated its 25 mm cannon for safety and flies a green flag to indicate "cold" (ceased firing) status. A yellow flag indicates a malfunction in a weapon, or the Bradley itself. *US Army photo courtesy Department of Defense*

TM 9-2350-284-PCL*

COMBAT VEHICLE
PRE-COMBAT CHECKLIST FOR:
FIGHTING VEHICLE, INFANTRY
M2A2 (2350-01-248-7619)
AND
FIGHTING VEHICLE, CAVALRY
M3A2 (2350-01-248-7620)

WARNING

THIS CHECKLIST IS TO BE USED ONLY WHEN AUTHORIZED BY THE COMMANDER. IT IS NOT INTENDED TO BE USED IN PLACE OF THE PMCS.

NOTE

THIS CHECKLIST CONTAINS CHECKS TO BE PERFORMED BEFORE COMBAT TO ASSURE VEHICLE IS MISSION CAPABLE. THE CHECKLIST SEQUENCE NUMBERS HEREIN CORRESPOND TO THOSE PMCS CHECKS IN TM 9-2350-284-10-1 AND TM 9-2350-284-10-2. REPORT CHECK RESULTS TO YOUR IMMEDIATE LEADER.

DISTRIBUTION STATEMENT A. Approved for public release; distribution is unlimited.

By Order of the Secretary of the Army

CARL E. VUONO
General, United States Army
Chief of Staff

Official:

PATRICIA P. HICKERSON
Colonel, United States Army
The Adjutant General

Distribution:

To be distributed in accordance with DA Form 12-37-E, Block 1954, Operator Maintenance Requirements for TM 9-2350-284-PCL.

DEPARTMENT OF THE ARMY
5 FEBRUARY 1991

* (Supersedes TM 9-2350-284-PCL, 8 March 1990)

☆ U. S. GOVERMENT PRINTING OFFICE : 1991 - 543-971

TM 9-2350-284-10-1

1.   **VEHICLE EXTERIOR:** Walk-Around And Check For Fluid Leaks, Obvious Damage, Tampering And Missing Parts That Prevent Operation.

*****NOTE: LOWER RAMP*****

2, 6.   **FINAL DRIVE AND HULL DRAIN PLUG FRONT:** Right And Left Final Drive Drain Plugs Installed And Close Front Drain.

7, 9.   **FIRE EXTINGUISHER SYSTEM FRONT:** Check Bottle Pressure And DISCH Light Is Off.

10, 11.   **ENGINE/INSTRUMENTS:** Start Engine And Check Instruments.

13.   **COMMUNICATION SYSTEM:** Radio and Intercom Operational.

16.   **HULL DRAIN PLUG REAR:** Close Rear Drain Plug.

17-19.   **FIRE EXTINGUISHER SYSTEM REAR:** Check Bottle Pressure.

TM 9-2350-284-10-2

*****POWER UP ISU*****

11, 12.   **COMMANDER/GUNNER CONTROL HANDLES:** Gun Elevation And Turret Traverse Operational.

FIRE CONTROL SYSTEM CHECKS

14.   **ISU**
15.   **25MM Gun.**
16.   **Coaxial Machine Gun.**
17.   **TOW System.**

47.   **NBC SYSTEM CHECK.**

PIN: 067530-000

United States General Accounting Office

GAO

Report to the Chairman, Subcommittee on
Regulation, Business Opportunities, and
Energy, Committee on Small Business,
House of Representatives

January 1992

OPERATION DESERT STORM

Early Performance Assessment of Bradley and Abrams

GAO/NSIAD-92-94

The Battle of Norfolk, February 1991. A Task Force 1-42 Bradley rolls past a destroyed Iraqi armored vehicle after one of the Army's largest tank battles since World War II. "The Bradley's TOW missile system," concluded a report to Congress, "was lethal against all forms of enemy armor ... crews reported destroying tanks at ranges from 800 to 3,700 meters." Tragically, seventeen out of the twenty Bradleys destroyed in the war were lost to friendly fire. As the GAO report put it, the Bradley was, "able to see and hit targets at greater ranges than it was able to positively identify targets." The Army incorporated Gulf War lessons learned into the M2A2/M3A2 ODS (Operation Desert Storm) versions, with improved crew survivability, communication, and navigation, including a Digital Compass System (DCS), Driver's Vision Enhancer Night Sight (DVE), Bradley Eyesafe Laser Range Finder (BELRF), and the then-revolutionary on-board Portable Lightweight GPS Receiver (PLGR, or "Plugger."). *US Army photo courtesy Department of Defense*

This 1992 General Accounting Office (GAO) report to Congress found that, in stark contrast to years' worth of media critics' dire predictions that the Bradley would be a failure in combat, it enjoyed very high readiness rates throughout the "Hundred Hour War:" 89% to 92% of the older "A-Zero" and M2A1/M3A1 models were consistently combat ready, while 92% to 96% of the newer M2A2/M3A2 models were able to "shoot, move, and communicate" when needed. *Photo courtesy author's collection*

This M2 IFV at Ft. Benning, undergoing maintenance while the author was researching this book, impressively "stopped on a dime" when parked in front of him. Notice the mixture of Desert Sand and 1980s forest green paint. Three hinged, lower side armor skirts or "armored aprons" have been raised up here, for access to the vehicle's suspension. Some crews also do this with the rearmost skirt, to avoid buildup of mud and rocks, which can cause the skirt to come off. *Photo courtesy National Armor and Cavalry Heritage Foundation*

Ft. Stewart, October 1993. 3rd Battalion, 7th Infantry Regiment, 24th Infantry Division M2A2s are loaded onto flatcars for deployment to Somalia. Notice 24th ID tactical "V" symbol on the rear troop door of closest IFV, and the variety of colors (dark green/tan) of the canvas protective covers on the TOW launchers—scale modelers note, after leaving the factory, Desert Sand vehicles don't always get issued perfectly matching Desert Sand replacement parts! *Photo by Don Teft courtesy US National Archives*

The US Cavalry leads the way. On December 31, 1995, a Bradley of NATO's Implementation Force (IFOR) leads Humvees across an Army-built pontoon bridge from Croatia into Bosnia, and the NATO base at Tuzla. Bradley crewmen train to drive with closed hatches (because the open hatch can interfere with traversing the main gun), but often disregard this for better visibility. The author later helped patrol the Bosnia-Croatian border with SFOR 12 in 2002–2003. *Photo by SRA Littlejohn courtesy US National Archives*

A Bosnian woman with an IFOR Bradley, 1996. Note atypically bright-colored dust caps on smoke grenade launchers, and rolled-up "swimming skirt" on the front slope. As the author learned while serving in Bosnia in 2002–2003, rural roads are narrow, unfinished, and potentially strewn with landmines and booby traps—as seen here, GIs allowed local civilians to lead the way, hoping they would not willfully walk into a mined area. *Photo courtesy US Army Military History Institute*

Operation Joint Endeavor, Bosnia. A 1/1 Cavalry Regiment, 1st Armor Division Bradley slogs through the ice and snow of a typical Bosnian winter, February 1996. *US Army photo by Staff Sgt. Jon Long courtesy US National Archives*

Serbian police look on as GIs use a Bradley and barbed wire to set up a hasty roadblock/checkpoint near the town of Brcko, Bosnia-Herzegovina, the scene of bitter fighting during the breakup of Yugoslavia. The author later served around Brcko in 2002–2003, during his Apache Troop (Forward), 1/104th Cavalry's service with NATO's SFOR 12. *Photo courtesy NATO*

At Hill 425, a remote area in rural Bosnia, an M3 CFV protects an American observation post in June 1996. "22 IFOR" is a square metal sign mounted on the Bradley's turret rear for quick identification. During the author's later Bosnia service, many rural sites were still more accessible by helicopter than by road; at upper left corner is a UH-60 Blackhawk. *US Army photo by Specialist Teresa Hawkins courtesy US National Archives*

Bosnia, June 1996. Standing next to an M3, a Task Force Eagle commander visits GIs at Hill 425, a remote signal site. *US Army photo by Specialist Teresa Hawkins courtesy US National Archives*

New Year's Day 1996. Serbian threats notwithstanding, after Army combat Engineers built one of the longest pontoon bridges in military history, Bradleys rolled across the Sava River and into Bosnia-Herzegovina. America's contribution to the Implementation Force (IFOR), Task Force Eagle, included some 20,000 troops. To the author, a veteran of NATO's later SFOR, this image evokes the typically harsh Bosnian winter conditions that American troops operated in. *Photo by Robert Ward, courtesy US Department of Defense*

Operation Joint Endeavor, February 1996. Ironically, American soldiers trained to fight Soviet AFVs and IFVs (including the author) ended up carrying out joint "presence patrols" with them in Bosnia-Herzegovina. Here, near Zvornik, Serbia, the crew of a 3rd Cavalry Regiment M2A2—still in Desert Storm–style Desert Sand paint—fraternizes with Russian Army soldiers in a BTR-80. *Photo courtesy US Army Military History Institute*

At the Port of Savannah, Georgia, Bradleys are lined up for loading onto the US Navy cargo ship USNS *Antares*, for delivery to Operation Bright Star 1997 wargames in Egypt. *Photo by Don Teft, courtesy US National Archives*

A poor quality but dramatic video camera still of the notorious "Brcko Riots" of August 1997, during which American peacekeepers (including GIs from the 2-2 Infantry), part of NATO's Operation Joint Guard, used Bradleys to defuse a tense situation with rioting Serbs. Author later served around Brcko with SFOR 12. *Photo courtesy GlobalSecurity.org*

October 1998. These M2s from the 2/9th Infantry, based at Camp Casey, South Korea, are about to cross the Imjin River on a pontoon bridge. *Photo by USAF Technical Sergeant James Mossman, courtesy US National Archives*

Crossing the Imjin, October 1998. Another 2/9th Infantry M2 on a pontoon bridge built by the Army's 50th Engineers. Vehicle loading markings are chalked on the side, and the troop door is open for ventilation. *US Air Force photo by Technical Sergeant James Mossman*

In the steep hills of South Korea, C Troop, 4th Squadron, 7th Cavalry Regiment Bradleys roll towards a live fire gunnery range in October 1998. *Photo by USAF Technical Sergeant James Mossman, courtesy US National Archives*

Stublina, Kosovo, March 2000. A Bradley keeps watch near the Serbian border as KFOR soldiers conduct weapons searches in the village below—notice TOW missile in firing position. KFOR later claimed that twenty-two crates of rifles, land mines, hand grenades, and small arms ammunition had been collected at five locations. In 2000, the Army introduced the M2A3/M3A3 Bradley variant, with advanced, fully digital electronics, including flat-panel information displays for the driver, commander, and squad in the rear compartment. *Photo courtesy US Department of Defense*

Operation Iraqi Freedom (OIF). Patrolling near Tikrit in February 2005, this Bradley sports Explosive Reactive Armor (ERA) tiles, added to improve crew protection from enemy High Explosive Anti-Tank (HEAT) rounds and Rocket Propelled Grenades (RPGs). Although commonly associated with OIF, M2A2/M3A2 ODS models equipped with bolt-on "ERA kits"—comprising about 105 reactive armor tiles or plates for the turret, sides, and hull—began to be fielded in Europe around the summer of 2000. *US Army photo courtesy Department of Defense*

Babil, Iraq, March 2005. A 2nd Battalion, 11th Armored Cavalry Regiment Bradley moves forward during a raid on the Hateen Weapons Complex. In a nod to the 1980s gangster movie "Scarface," the artwork on the TOW launcher reads, "Say hello to my little friend!" *US Navy photo by CPM Edward Martens*

FIELD MANUAL 3-22.1 (FM 23-1)

BRADLEY GUNNERY

In a digital age, with the prevalence of the Internet and camera phones, the enemy was quick to circulate photos of burning or destroyed American equipment. *Photo courtesy Tumbler.com*

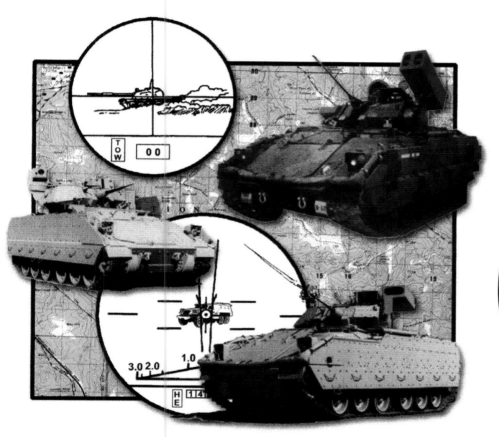

NOVEMBER 2003

HEADQUARTERS, DEPARTMENT OF THE ARMY

Operation Beastmaster. Bradleys take up a blocking position near Baghdad in December 2006. *US Army photo*

An 8th Infantry Regiment platoon leader talks under the watchful eye of a Bradley during a joint coalition forces clearing operation near Mosul, Iraq, in April 2008. Notice the use of the large camouflage net to provide sunshade and some concealment from snipers. *US Army photo by Sgt. John Crosby*

This Bradley at Camp Beuhring, Kuwait—shown in October 2010, during 4th Infantry Division gunnery training—gives a good view of the mounts on the front and side for extra, "bolt-on" armor tiles and boxes. Notice the orange tint of the driver's vision blocks, a protective coating to resist enemy attempts at blinding the driver. *US Army photo by PFC Khori Johnson*

South Korea, June 2011. After arriving on the USS *Watson*, these new M2A2 IFVs and M3A3 CFVs are loaded onto railcars in Pusan for delivery to the Second Infantry Division. The TOW launcher tubes are protected from dirt and dust by a simple green fabric cover. *US Army photo by SPC Bryan Willis*

These Bradleys from the 22nd Infantry Regiment, 4th Infantry Division are being loaded up at the Kuwait Naval Base, Kuwait, in March 2013, during an exercise to determine logistical requirements for rapid deployment. *US Army photo by Sgt. William Henry*

Gunnery Training, Ft. Hood, Texas. An 8th Cavalry Regiment, 1st Cavalry Division Bradley fires its 25 mm Bushmaster in June 2013. The Bradley's height comes across here, in contrast to Soviet-designed BMPs and BTRs, which have a relatively low profile. *US Army photo by PFC Paige Pendleton*

Combined Resolve II. In May 2014, 2nd Battalion, 5th Cavalry Regiment Bradleys roll out of the Hohenfels, Germany, training base for this multinational training exercise. Typically, there would be four M2s in a mechanized infantry platoon, thirteen per company, and forty-one per battalion. Prominent on the leading vehicle, in front of the commander's hatch, is a Desert Sand-colored Transparent Armor Gun Shield (TAGS). *US Army photo by Capt. John Farmer*

Humvee, Abrams, Bradley. A trio designed to work together in the 1970s and 1980s, soldiers on in August 2015, during a 3rd Armored Brigade Combat Team Field Training eXercise (FTX) at the Udairi Range Complex, Kuwait. *US Army photo by Staff Sgt. Grady Jones*

Decades ago, the Bradley's designers anticipated survivability upgrades as needed, using "bolt-on" additions. As the Iraq War ground on and the threat of RPGs and snipers grew, extra equipment such as Explosive Reactive Armor (ERA) tiles, boxes, and modules, enhanced crew weapons stations, and Transparent Armor Gun Shields (TAGS) were added, all of which worsened the vehicle's already clunky, ungraceful appearance. *US Army photo courtesy Department of Defense*

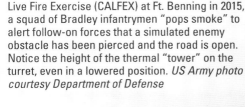

Warthog! Bradleys (along with their stable mate, the M1 Abrams tank) enjoy close air support from the A-10 Thunderbolt II, affectionately known as the "Warthog." In November 2015, a "Hog" flies over 3rd Infantry Division elements during live-fire weapons training at the Army's Grafenwoehr Training Area. *US Army photo by Major Randy Ready*

Once more unto the breach: At a Combined Arms Live Fire Exercise (CALFEX) at Ft. Benning in 2015, a squad of Bradley infantrymen "pops smoke" to alert follow-on forces that a simulated enemy obstacle has been pierced and the road is open. Notice the height of the thermal "tower" on the turret, even in a lowered position. *US Army photo courtesy Department of Defense*

Fort Irwin, 2015. Bradley crews appreciate the AH-64 Apache helicopter gunship, which supports them by scouting the route ahead and—if needed—taking on enemy armor with Hellfire missiles. While serving in Bosnia, the author found the presence of Apaches like this one (supporting 1st Cavalry Division troops at the National Training Center) overhead to be reassuring, an ever-watchful "eye in the sky." *US Army photo by Sgt. Richard Jones*

At the National Training Center in 2015, ground guides with fluorescent PT belts prepare to lead 2nd Armored Brigade Combat Team, 1st Infantry Division Bradleys into Operation Decisive Action Rotation 15-06. According to the Army, this wargame pits soldiers against "an adaptable enemy force, in an austere and fluctuating environment." *US Army photo by Sgt. Richard Jones*

This M3A3 at Ft. Stewart in March 2016, exemplifies the Bradley's "ugly duckling" appearance. The black rubber brush guard on the side armor—usually hooked to the second skirt from the front and often seen carrying plastic 5-gallon water cans—covers strapped-on crew gear such as rucksacks or sleeping bags, to keep them from being torn off while driving through rough terrain. Directly above the brush guard is the prominent commander's thermal vision tower. *US Army photo by PFC Payton Wilson*

Bradleys can be transported worldwide by C-5, C-17, and C-141 aircraft, as well as "roll-on, roll-off" cargo ships. Here, a cargo specialist watches over a Bradley as it leaves the hull of the USNS *Brittin* at the Port of Shuaiba, Kuwait, March 2017. *US Army photo by Leticia Hopkins*

Alexandria, Louisiana, November 2015. During Operation Green Flag Little Rock, a Bradley is loaded by soldiers into a C-17 Globemaster transport plane. The hinged side skirts have been lifted up for access to the suspension and road wheels. *US Air Force photo by Senior Airman Scott Poe*

Soldiers and airmen secure a Bradley inside the cargo hold of a C-17 Globemaster for use in the Green Flag Little Rock training exercise, November 2015. *US Air Force photo by Senior Airman Scott Poe*

Operation Atlantic Resolve, Zagan, Poland. As the sun rises over the Karliki range in February 2017, 3rd Armored Brigade Combat Team Bradleys attached to the 4th Infantry Division are ready to roll into live fire exercises.
US Army photo by Spc. Emily Houdershieldt

Off into the sunset. Dismounted Army "19 Deltas" (the Military Occupational Specialty, or MOS, for Cavalry scouts) patrol with their Bradleys close at hand at Ft. Hunter Liggett, California, in June 2015. After a controversial start, the Bradley has served faithfully in multiple wars and peacekeeping operations for over three decades. *US Army photo courtesy Department of Defense*

In late 2016, BAE systems showed off its "Next Generation Bradley" concept vehicle, featuring many improvements such as a redesigned, blast-resistant hull and suspension, relocated fuel tanks to improve crew protection from mines and IEDs, more electrical power and horsepower, and an upgraded M2A4 standard turret with advanced electronics such as jammers and Active Protection Systems (APS). The Bradley is scheduled to continue into service into the 2030s. *Photo courtesy BAE Systems*

CHAPTER 3
Men, Machines, Guns, and Gear: The Bradley in Detail

An M3 Cavalry Fighting Vehicle (CFV) built in 1983, and now on display at Ft. Benning, Georgia. Notice the relatively sleek, uncluttered appearance of the early Bradley, when compared to today's variants with additional armor, antennas, weapons stations, etc. A quick recognition feature to distinguish M2s and M3s is that the CFV lacks the crew firing ports seen on the side of the M2 IFV. *Photo courtesy National Armor and Cavalry Heritage Foundation*

It can be confusing to sort out the multitude of Bradley variants in a photo taken from a distance. This chapter features closer views of some of those hatches, boxes, handles, covers, doors, etc., on the Bradley, and explains what they're for. The vehicle has changed throughout its history, receiving modifications and improvements from "Operation Desert Storm" (ODS) armor in 1991, to "TAGS," "BRATs," etc. in the present Afghanistan and Iraq Wars.

Many civilians are unaware that to run an armored fighting vehicle in the field for a few short hours requires many further hours of inspections, basic maintenance, safety checks, etc., as any soldier who has performed a "BII inspection" (emptying the vehicle of every tool and accessory, or Basic Issue, and laying them on the ground for a detailed inspection), can attest. Track tension must be checked and adjusted, fluid levels confirmed and adjusted, barrels swabbed out before and after firing, sights and computers checked and fine tuned, before the Bradley can roll out of the motor pool or Forward Observation Base (FOB).

The Bradley has undergone quite an evolution during its service life; there are stark visual differences when one compares photos of an early M2 or M3 of 1983 or so to today's latest, Frankenstein-monster-like variants overloaded with unsightly, "bolt-on" modifications. But this is a testament to the essential soundness of the "IFV/CFV" design; the M2/M3 series has constantly evolved—not always painlessly—but still evolved to meet the changing battlefield, expanded enemy threats, and new technology like GPS and digital communication.

While the early road was rough, decades after being damned as a "Dud," "Moving Target," and "Billion Dollar Death Trap" by a hostile media, the Bradley rolls on into its fourth decade of service. Today, in contrast to the damning epitaphs of the past, it's now known affectionately by the American soldiers who crew it by a plain, down-to-earth name: the simple, dependable "Brad."

Crew compartment of an M3 CFV. Seating just two cavalry scouts, it has more room for ammunition stowage than the IFV version. In the center is the turret base, with the shield door unlatched and slid into the open position. On the floor of both Bradley models are removable plates to stow seven (IFV) or eight (CFV) boxes of 25 mm ammunition. Note M16 rifles on left, below ammo racks, and TOW missiles on right. Although many prior US armored fighting vehicle interiors had been painted bright white, the Bradley's is a light mint green, less visible to an enemy when the rear ramp is down. *US Army photo by SPC Diana Lindsey, courtesy National Archives*

An M3 CFV of the 63rd Armored Regiment, attached to the Third Infantry Division in mid-1980s, Cold War Germany. The small turret bustle rack did not allow for much storage, so GIs strapped their gear all over the vehicle. *1/35 scale model and photo by author*

The M242 Bushmaster 25 mm gun on an early M3 CFV, fed by a metallic link belt, could rapidly fire armor piercing (AP) or high explosive (HE) ammunition at ranges up to 3,000 meters. The M240 coaxial machine gun (left of main gun) is not installed on this vehicle, hence the absence of a protruding 7.62 mm barrel from the "shroud." In addition to the external vane sight used to quickly align guns with targets, the commander has a backup "ring sight" to help track flying aircraft. *Photo courtesy National Armor and Cavalry Heritage Foundation*

The Bradley's off-center "clamshell" driver's hatch allowed for better visibility and more comfortable driving, while the flat trim vane on the front slope allowed for gear stowage. The orange "67" on the side is a tactical marking used during 1980s Cold War wargames, made of paper and attached with GI issue green duct tape. *1/35 scale model and photo by author*

Ramp down, January 1985. Another M2 Bradley IFV during Operation Reforger in West Germany. At that time, a typical Infantry squad carried by the vehicle consisted of six men—four riflemen, an M60 machine gunner, and a machine gun loader/ammo bearer. In 1986, the M2A1/M3A1 variant was introduced, featuring the more powerful TOW II antitank missile, improved Nuclear/Biological Chemical (NBC) protection, and external changes such as a larger turret bustle rack able to hold more crew stowage. *US Army photo courtesy Department of Defense*

A Second Armored Division M2 Bradley driver at Ft. Hood, 1986. Notice the periscopes above him, used for closed-hatch driving. *Photo by William Rosenmund, courtesy US National Archives*

The bent back, tied down whip radio antennas (to avoid hitting power lines) and the relatively clean lines when compared to subsequent variants give this 1980s Cold War M3 CFV a rakish look. *1/35 scale model and photo by author*

A 41st Infantry Regiment GI in the gunner's position of an M2, Ft. Hood, 1986. The lack of protective goggles on his CVC helmet is uncommon. Note the position of the smoke grenade boxes to the right of the cannon, which was changed on later variants. *Photo by William Rosenmund, courtesy US National Archives*

This Bradley infantryman's weapon in January 1986, reminds us of the vehicle's long service life—he is armed with an M60 machine gun first fielded before the Vietnam War, and wears the classic M1 "steel pot" helmet little changed from its 1942 debut. The M2 behind him carries MILES gear on the cannon barrel. *Photo by William Rosenmund, courtesy US National Archives*

Gear up. Before the advent of the Army's Battle Dress Utilities (BDUs) in the early 1980s, the first M2/M3 crews wore solid green, OG 507–colored uniforms. At top left is a late-1970s issue Combat Vehicle Crewman (CVC) helmet with goggles and flexible extension cord. Below the CVC is a 1985-dated Bradley "Dash Ten" (technical manual), often carried in the vehicle by crews. On the right, on top of a 1980-dated M65 field jacket, is a 1986-manufactured M1 "steel pot" helmet with fabric cover, a World War Two design that continued to be worn until replaced by the controversial Kevlar "Fritz" helmet. *Author photo*

Dismounted 1st Squadron/9th Cavalry Regiment 19 Deltas (Cavalry scouts) approach a Bradley during night training at the National Training Center, Ft. Irwin, California, in February 2015. While tankers are taught "death before dismount," Cavalry scouts are constantly moving in and out of the Bradley's troop compartment, to patrol on foot. Note the dim light inside the troop compartment, designed to provide illumination without disturbing night vision. *US Army photo by Sgt. Richard Jones*

This is a rare M3A0 ("A-Zero") CFV prototype, built in 1981, by Food Machinery and Chemical (FMC) Corporation. It was later used in the M7 BFIST test program (to develop a fire support variant of the Bradley), and eventually donated to Carlisle Barracks. *Photo courtesy US Army Heritage and Education Center, Carlisle Barracks, Pennsylvania*

Germany, 1991. A 1st Armored Division M2A2 IFV crew shortly before deploying to Kuwait and Iraq, for Operations Desert Shield/Desert Storm. The M2A2 has a three-man crew of commander, gunner, and driver, plus an Infantry squad of six soldiers in the back. Debuting in 1988, the first 662 M2A2/M3A2s used the original 500 HP engine; after May 1989, successive vehicles rolled out with an improved, 600 HP Cummins VTA-903 engine and General Dynamics HMPT-500 transmission. Prominent external recognition features of the M2A2/M3A2 include the added crew protection (note 1¼″ thick side armor skirt behind the soldier), new armored engine cover with rolled-up water barrier or "skirt" used for fording, relocated headlights and smoke grenade stowage boxes, and the elimination of the M240 coax gun's "shroud" or cover. *Photo courtesy Sgt. Ron Whitehead*

HOW THEY FIGHT
DESERT SHIELD
ORDER OF BATTLE
HANDBOOK
September 1990

Typical Desert Storm gear, 1991. A tan-painted CVC helmet with goggles rests on a traditional Arab shemagh head scarf—very non-regulation but quickly adopted by practical GIs. The yellow booklet provides details on friendly and enemy armies likely to be encountered in the Persian Gulf, while the white card on the right is a "Pre-Combat Checklist" for Bradley crews. The leaflets were dropped on Iraqi troops to encourage surrender; the foremost one was cleverly disguised on one side as Iraqi currency to encourage its being picked up. *Author photo*

Desert Storm gear used by Bradley crews, 1991. An originally dark green CVC helmet, now repainted tan, rests along with souvenir surrender leaflets on a fabric cover for the PASGT (Personnel Armor System, Ground Troops) ballistic or "flak" vest. Because the body armor vest was produced in the Woodland Camouflage scheme more appropriate for Europe, GIs added these simple covers to blend into the desert. Although the DBDU (Desert Battle Dress Uniform) pattern—which soldiers likened to "chocolate chip cookie dough"— became an icon of the Persian Gulf War of 1991, American soldiers had been wearing it since the early 1980s.
Author photo

Medina Ridge, February 1991. A First Armored Division Bradley crew breaks out the cigars after the all-night battle, during which US VII Corps troops (including the 1st and 3rd Armored Divisions and 1st Infantry Division) took on elite Iraqi Republican Guards units. Abrams tanks and Bradley IFVs and CFVs, supported by AH-64 Apache gunships, not only foiled an attempted Iraqi ambush, they destroyed some 300 enemy vehicles. During the "100 Hour War," some Bradley crews received the new M919 round for the 25 mm Bushmaster, with a powerful, depleted uranium penetrator projectile.
By late February 1991, some 2,200 Bradleys were present in the Persian Gulf area, with frontline units and in reserve.
Approximately 692 were of the latest "A2" variant.
Photo courtesy US Army Military History Institute

During SPEARPOINT '84, part of Exercise REFORGER 1984 in West Germany, a GI of the 3rd Battalion, 67th Armor Regiment, works on the right final drive plate of his M2 Bradley IFV. *US Army photo by SPC5 Vincent Kitts*

The large, flat armored cover on the front slope of this M3A2 CFV at Ft. Knox swings up to reveal the transmission. The Cummins engine, to the driver's right, is powered by 175 gallons of JP-8 (Army diesel fuel), and has a range of about 300 miles. A combat-loaded Bradley can go from a full stop to 30 mph in about twenty seconds.
Photo by Chris Conners

This shot shows the Bradley's height in relation to a standing soldier. Acting as ground guides to park and position vehicles, GIs grow comfortable with walking and moving around them, and learn to trust their drivers and fellow crewmen. The round circle on the right side Bradley's rear ramp is a towing cable/rope. Notice exposed tubes at the rear of the TOW launchers; perhaps firing soon, the crews have removed the canvas cover that usually protects them from sand, dust, and debris.
Photo courtesy US Department of Defense

Looking into the troop compartment, standing on the rear ramp of an M3A3 CFV at Ft. Knox, Kentucky. At left, bench seating for troops; past the bench is a "tunnel" leading to the driver's compartment, which troops call the "hellhole." Access to the round gunner and track commander's turret is through the sliding door at center. The flat display screen in upper left corner conveys digital information to passengers while in motion. Note removable floor panels for ammo storage. *Photo by Chris Conners*

A wire rope and footstep on the side of the Bradley enables the crew to board and dismount. The wire loops are also used to secure gear to the Bradley's hull. *Photo courtesy US Army Heritage and Education Center, Carlisle Barracks, Pennsylvania*

Periscopes on an M2A3 driver's hatch. The orange tint is a lens coating designed to protect drivers from enemy lasers. Notice also the smoke grenade projectors, taken from a green-painted vehicle. *Photo by Richard Brian*

This Bradley driver, from the 2nd Battalion, 7th Infantry Regiment, wears goggles to protect him from the desert dust and sand of Ft. Irwin, California. From his position, the driver can mechanically raise and lower the large, armored access door (lower left) to perform basic crew maintenance in the field on the engine and transmission. The roll of barbed wire is a common sight on US vehicles, used to set up hasty checkpoints and roadblocks as needed. *US Army photo by Specialist Stephen Solomon*

Looking down into the driver's compartment of an M3A3 CFV at Ft. Knox, with the seat in the down or flat position. The rubber padding around the edge of the hatch gives some protection during sudden stops and exiting/entering the vehicle, and the thickness of the driver's armor protection can be seen. The black warning placard has information on starting the engine and operation in unusual conditions, like fording and swimming. The gray box in the lower left corner is the gearshift—the Bradley has one reverse and three forward gears. The large door to the driver's right holds spare parts and gun tools, while the black-tipped handle at center top is a lock for the rear ramp. *Photo by Chris Conners*

A Bradley and its crew (track commander on left, gunner on right) from the 2/9th Infantry based at Camp Casey, South Korea, are ferried across the Imjin River in October 1998. *Photo by USAF Technical Sergeant James Mossman, courtesy US National Archives*

Note subtly rounded hull side skirts on this M3 CFV at Ft. Benning. The flat rectangular panel above the headlights is the trim vane (later deleted on the M2A2/M2A3), which swings out and down for the crew to stand on while parked and performing basic maintenance on the engine, transmission, and main gun. Rarely, GIs kept it down while in motion, piled high with gear as a field expedient storage rack. *Photo courtesy National Armor and Cavalry Heritage Foundation*

Detail of front tracks and rubber fender on a Bradley of the 7th Infantry Regiment, 3rd Infantry Division, during gunnery training with Latvian forces in May 2015. Typical M2/M3 tracks are about 21 inches wide; early versions were replaced with a wider, longer-lasting model known as the "Big Foot," for better ground handling. M2A2/M2A3 variants also benefit from an improved drive sprocket and tracks first tested on the M270 Multiple Launch Rocket System (MLRS). *US Army photo by Staff Sgt. Brooks Fletcher*

From the M2A2/M3A2 forward, the headlights were redesigned, repositioned, and carried in a more robust housing. The clear light is the headlight, while the orange lens is a turn indicator. The dark rectangle beneath the turn indicator is a blackout marker light. *Photo courtesy US Army Heritage and Education Center, Carlisle Barracks, Pennsylvania*

Through the looking glass—a view through an M2A3's periscope of a Bradley camouflaged while parked with the usual net and poles. In accordance with the scouting and reconnaissance role of the US Cavalry, the M3A2 CFV's cargo hatch has more periscopes than the IFV version. *Photo by Richard Brian*

Grafenwoehr Training Area, Germany, June 2014. Troopers of the 5th Cavalry Regiment, 1st Brigade Combat Team, 1st Cavalry Division dismount and move out. "Graf" is known for Range 301, one of the largest and most modern live fire ranges in Europe. Notice the subtle "inverted Vee" tactical marking near the driver's position, probably made with GI "100 MPH" duct tape.
US Army photo by Captain John Farmer

Before the Army adopted NATO's three-color paint scheme in the mid-1980s, Bradleys like this M3 CFV were painted forest green. The first model turret bustle rack on the M2/M3, which slanted inward, was too cramped for adequate storage of GI's personal gear, but later enlarged. Often seen on the top center of the bustle rack is a square metal placard with "battle" or "tactical" (unit/vehicle) markings. The rectangular racks on turret rear hold GI cans of 7.62 mm ammunition for the gunner's and coaxial machine guns. *Photo courtesy National Armor and Cavalry Heritage Foundation*

While these circular bolts on an M3A0 serve a practical purpose—the attachment of bolt-on steel applique/ERA (Explosive Reactive Armor) to the vehicle—the profusion of lumps and bumps on the Bradley gives it an "ugly duckling" appearance. *Photo courtesy US Army Heritage and Education Center, Carlisle Barracks, Pennsylvania*

To keep up with Soviet advances in tank ammunition, anti-tank weapons, and AFV firepower, Bradleys from M2A2/M3A2 variants onward carried applique side skirt spaced armor, which GIs preparing to deploy to the Persian Gulf in 1990–91 dubbed "ODS (Operation Desert Storm) armor." Thanks to the foresight of the Bradley's designers in the 1970s—who included a "bolt-on" capability to upgrade the vehicle's armor—earlier models like this M3A0 could be brought up to the latest standard. *Photo courtesy US Army Heritage and Education Center, Carlisle Barracks, Pennsylvania*

"Fill her up and check the oil!" In Baghdad, Iraq, in April 2008, a 68th Armor Regiment, 4th Infantry Division Bradley crewman measures the engine oil level. *US Army photo by Sgt. Joseph Rebolledo*

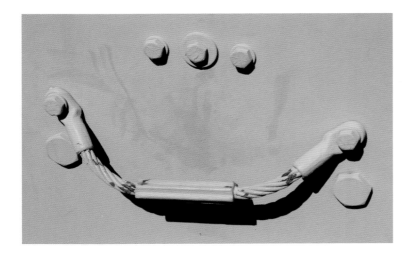

Close-up of one of the wire rope steps on the Bradley's side, used to mount and dismount and stow the crew's gear, such as backpacks, sleeping bags, and mats. *Photo courtesy US Army Heritage and Education Center, Carlisle Barracks, Pennsylvania*

This view shows the thickness of the spaced armor on the side skirts and engine/transmission cover. Notice the rough, non-stick finish on the cover, which soldiers appreciate when mounting/dismounting in rainy or snowy weather. *Photo courtesy US Army Heritage and Education Center, Carlisle Barracks, Pennsylvania*

Ft. Irwin, California, August 2014. Before moving out, the powered engine/transmission cover is raised for basic Preventive Maintenance Checks and Services (PMCS), such as checking fluid levels, on this 2nd Battalion, 7th Infantry Regiment Bradley. The cover's flat surface makes a convenient storage space for rolls of barbed wire used to set up hasty checkpoints. *US Army photo by Spec. Stephen Solomon*

A sergeant of the 1st Cavalry Regiment, 5th Infantry Division displays a belt of dummy 25 mm training rounds used in the Bradley at Ft. Polk, Louisiana in April 1990. *US Army photo by SPC Diana Lindsay courtesy National Archives*

Designed to be removed and replaced relatively quickly, the Bradley's self-contained engine and transmission are known together as the "power pack." The Cummins VTA-903 turbo-charged diesel engine of the M2/M3 produced 500 horsepower, while the later VTA-903T (used in the M2A2/M3A2) increased this to 600 HP. Able to reach around 40 mph cross-country, the Bradley can keep up with M1 Abrams-series tanks. Here, a mechanic services a Bradley engine at Combat Outpost Summers, Iraq, in July 2008. *US Army photo by Sgt. David Turner*

The Bradley's 25 mm M242 Chain Gun can be elevated to 60 degrees and depressed to 10. Its "interlock" safety feature prevents the gun from firing when it is too close to the troop hatch on rear deck, or if the driver's or cargo hatches are open past the "pop-up" position. It also has a latch near the mantlet or rotor extension (at the base of the main gun), used to quickly replace the barrel. *Photo courtesy US Army Heritage and Education Center, Carlisle Barracks, Pennsylvania*

The electrically fired smoke grenade projectors—
here located on the left and right front of an
M3A0's turret—can fire a total of eight smoke
grenades at the same time, creating a "curtain"
of smoke to help obscure the vehicle. Extra
grenades are stored in stowage bins on both
sides of the 25 mm gun, and the launchers are
often covered with a black rubber cap (not seen
here) to keep out dust and debris. On the bottom
two launchers can be seen tiny drain holes, that
can be cleaned out using pipe cleaners. *Photo
courtesy US Army Heritage and Education Center,
Carlisle Barracks, Pennsylvania*

The first Bradleys weighed approximately
twenty-five tons. Using their tracks for propulsion,
they could "swim" at 4 mph with a trim vane and
swimming skirt. But as later models gained
weight from armored side skirts, reactive armor
boxes and tiles, etc. (the "-A2" variants jumped to
thirty-two tons, and a "full suite" of armor tiles
alone adds as much as 8,000 additional pounds),
the improved crew survivability degraded the
vehicle's amphibious capability. If river crossings
are necessary, the Army has pontoon bridges
(such as the one built by combat Engineers to
cross the Sava River into Bosnia) and folding
bridge vehicles. On the armored engine cover of
this 1st Battalion, 156th Infantry Regiment
Bradley, seen in Iraq, in February 2007, are the
inverted "W"-shaped brackets used to mount
Bradley Reactive Armor Tile (BRAT) modules, not
yet installed. *US Army photo by SGM Steven
Stuckey*

During a June 2008 "air/ground integration training event" at Ft. Hood, Texas, Col. Douglas Gabram, a 1st Cavalry Division AH-64 Apache pilot, takes an orientation ride in the track commander's seat of an M2A3. *US Army photo by Staff Sgt. Nathan Hoskins*

A view from the track commander's seat of an M3A3 at Ft. Knox. The flat screen displays info on friendly and enemy locations, and can send and receive it to and from other vehicles. The black handle with red button (top right) is the TC's "Cadillac," or override control, which he can use to elevate or traverse the cannon to help put his gunner on target. Two periscope vision blocks are seen above the flat screen. Below the screen are controls for the Commander's Independent Thermal Viewer (CITV) and laser ranger finder, to adjust the view mode, power, polarity, etc. *Photo by Chris Conners*

In front of the track commander's (TC's) hatch on an M3A0 CFV is his external gunsight, linked to the 25 mm Bushmaster's barrel by this pivoting arm. Lining up an open ring and a clear reticle with crosshairs, the TC can track targets such as low-flying aircraft. *Photo courtesy US Army Heritage and Education Center, Carlisle Barracks, Pennsylvania*

Night sights on thermal: the black rectangle at center left, below coaxial gun, is one of the periscope vision blocks. Each has a blackout cover, activated from inside the turret, to prevent interior lighting from being seen from outside the vehicle. Heat appears as white, cool objects as black. *US Army photo courtesy Department of Defense*

Newer versions of the Bushmaster's barrel have a rust-resistant chrome lining. Notice the tapered, fluted shape. The approximate total weight of the gun system on the Bradley (receiver, barrel, and feeder) is just 243 pounds, which seems light to an old M1A1 Abrams tanker like the author. *Photo courtesy US Army Heritage and Education Center, Carlisle Barracks, Pennsylvania*

Bradley crewmen of the 7th Infantry Regiment, 3rd Infantry Division lay out belts of 25 mm ammo for the vehicle's Bushmaster cannon during live fire exercises at Ft. Bragg, North Carolina. A typical Bradley IFV carries about 900 rounds (300 readily accessible; 600 stored in the hull) for the Bushmaster, and 2,200 rounds (800 at the ready; 1,400 stored in the hull) for the coaxial machine gun. *US Army photo by Spc. Wyatt Davis*

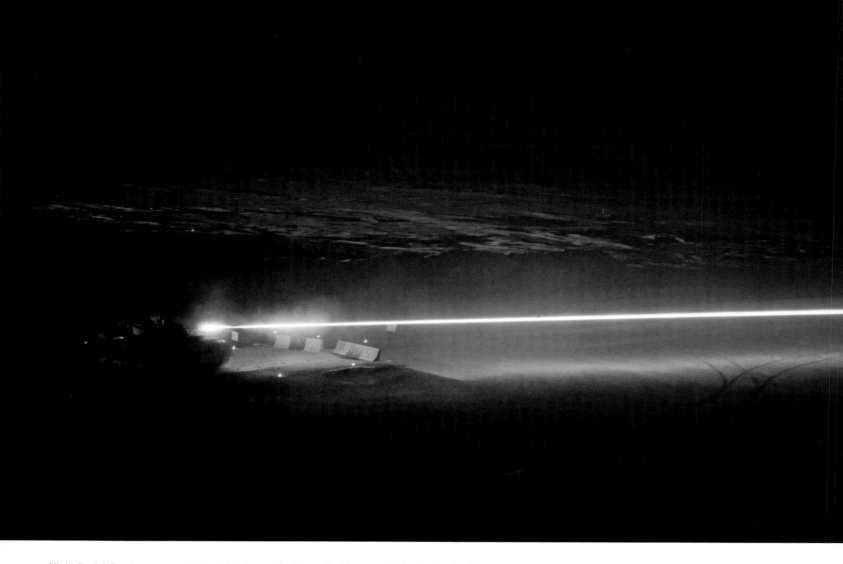

Night fire! A Bradley crew with the 8th Infantry Regiment, 2nd Armored Brigade Combat Team, 4th Infantry Division qualifies on "Table Six" gunnery testing at the Udairi Range, Kuwait, in January 2014. *US Army photo by SGT Marcus Fichtl.*

Spent ammunition brass and links fall out of the large, cut-out area on the bottom right of the turret, to be collected by the crew if possible. *US Army photo courtesy Department of Defense.*

The integral crew door in the hydraulically operated rear ramp of this M3A0 allows manual ingress/egress, even if the ramp should become jammed, or its hydraulics fail. Notice square firing port for M321 Firing Port Weapon (FPW) above the door handle. *Photo courtesy US Army Heritage and Education Center, Carlisle Barracks, Pennsylvania.*

Ft. Hood, October 2014. Seated in the rear troop compartment, an instructor trains Army MOS 19 Deltas (Cavalry scouts) of B Troop, 6th Squadron, 9th Cavalry Regiment, 1st Cavalry Division how to evacuate a Bradley during fire or rollover. At lower left corner are the ever-present plastic GI five-gallon water cans. *US Army photo by Sgt. Quentin Johnson*

An M321 Firing Port Weapon (FPW), mounted in the troop compartment's rear door. The initial Bradley concept envisioned troops using the FPW to actively fight from inside the vehicle while on the move, and M2 IFVs had six firing ports on the sides and rear. The side ports were plated over on subsequent variants, covered by enhanced armor, reactive armor tiles and boxes, etc. While later Bradley IFV variants retain the rear firing port in the ramp door, it was deleted from the M3A2. *Photo courtesy Department of Defense*

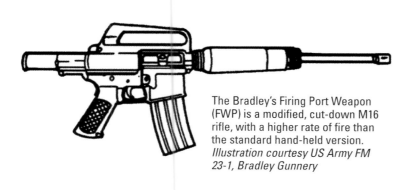

The Bradley's Firing Port Weapon (FWP) is a modified, cut-down M16 rifle, with a higher rate of fire than the standard hand-held version. *Illustration courtesy US Army FM 23-1, Bradley Gunnery*

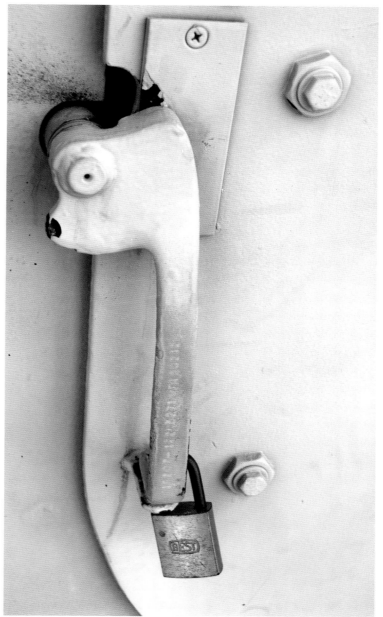

The rear crew door is secured in Army motor pools with a common brass padlock—in Army parlance, formally designated NSN 5340-00-682-1645, the "Padlock, Brass or Bronze, Key Operated, W/2 Keys." *Photo courtesy US Army Heritage and Education Center, Carlisle Barracks, Pennsylvania*

November 2004. The large square plate on the turret rear of this M3A2 shows unit and vehicle information, or "battle markings," for quick identification. Note the armor thickness of the rear hatch's integral door, and the prominent ERA armor boxes above the spaced armor on the vehicle's side. *US Army photo by SSG Shane Cuomo, courtesy National Archives*

Close-up of a road wheel on an M3A0. Crewmen check fluid levels through the clear plastic sight glass (in the middle of the hub) and add more as needed through the filler plugs. *Photo courtesy US Army Heritage and Education Center, Carlisle Barracks, Pennsylvania*

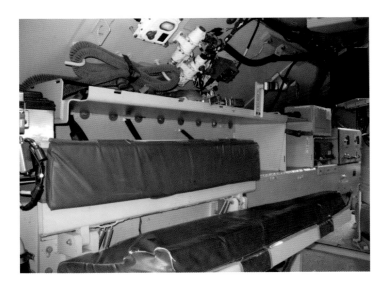

Looking into an M3A3's rear compartment, left side. The interior layout of Bradley has repeatedly changed; for example, the M3A3 deleted the front and rear-facing scout seats used in the M3. From left, folding bench seats for 19 Deltas (cavalry scouts), ammo box storage above the bench, and a white square, dimmable cabin light. Note red manual fire extinguisher, green air-filtration hose, and green square "J-Box" (junction box), for soldiers to connect their CVC helmets. Flat display screen in upper right shows digital info while on the move. Open tunnel on lower right leads to the driver's compartment. *Photo by Chris Conners*

Looking inside and to the right in an M3A2 CFV, which has a crew of three, plus two scouts in the rear compartment. Notice the large troop hatch (top) used to reload the TOW missiles in open position. The partially red stowage racks are for TOW missiles. The Bradley has also carried Javelin, Dragon, and AT-4 missiles, steadily upgraded to match the capabilities of Soviet-bloc light armor. The large red tube below the cabin light is a hand-held Halon fire extinguisher. *Photo by Chris Conners*

While teaching 7th Cavalry Regiment, 3rd Infantry Division GIs during Exercise Combined Resolve VI at Hohenfels, Germany, in May 2016, Timberwolves Observer Coaches (umpires) take a break inside a Bradley troop compartment. Small, desert tan Combat Identification Panels (CIPs) have been added to the doors of the rear stowage boxes. Stowed on the floor, under the right side bench, is a case of Army Meals, Ready to Eat (MREs).
US Army photo by Sgt. Alexandra Hulett

The interior of an M2A3 with the rear ramp down and overhead troop hatch open. Typical "squad seating" is three men per side, on folding benches, as seen here. Bright red canisters are manually operated Halon fire extinguishers, should the automatic fire suppression system fail. Notice the GI seated in the gunner's position. *Photo by Richard Brian*

The two hinged storage boxes on the rear of the Bradley (here, an early M3 CFV at Ft. Benning) are secured by black rubber toggle handles, and can hold hand grenades, mines, flares, rations, ammo boxes, commo wire, even a small GI stove. The M3 CFV's interior holds three crewmen and two cavalry scouts in the rear, while the M2 IFV carries three crewmen and six squad members. *Photo courtesy National Armor and Cavalry Heritage Foundation*

Going in. An M3A2 will typically have a three-man crew (driver, gunner, track commander) and six GIs in the rear. The M3 CFV series, intended for Cavalry reconnaissance and scouting roles, carries fewer soldiers (two 19 Deltas, or cavalry scouts) in the crew compartment, and more ammunition. *US Army photo courtesy Department of Defense*

This Iraq War M3A3 CFV of the 2nd Squadron, 3rd Armored Cavalry Regiment (2/3rd ACR), attached to the 2nd Infantry Division, shows the "full suite" of explosive reactive armor (ERA) tiles and boxes that can be added to increase protection. Note also the Commander's Independent Thermal Viewer (CITV) and added ballistic glass protection around the track commander's (TC's) position. While unsightly, the extra protection necessitated by urban combat and the IED threat in Afghanistan and Iraq is a credit to the Bradley's designers, who foresaw a "bolt-on" capability for improved protection back in the 1970s. *1/35 model and photo by author*

Muqdadiyah, Iraq. A dramatic example of how, while unsightly, some of the recent "bolt-on" additions to the already awkward-looking Bradley save soldiers' lives. In January 2006, this turret glass absorbed shrapnel from a 155 mm Improvised Explosive Device (IED). *US Army photo by Staff Sgt. Mark Wojciechowski*

Move out! An infantry squad hurries out of a Bradley's rear troop compartment. The first few seconds of exiting the vehicle and running into the unknown can be tense. *Photo courtesy Department of Defense*

An interesting nighttime view, through thermal sights, of a Bradley on the move. Because the night sights used highly cooled circuits, they typically require a few minutes to warm up for best performance. Given the shining light coming from the Bradley and the walking soldier's relaxed posture in this photo, it's likely that the vehicle is being "ground guided" into an American base. *US Army photo courtesy Department of Defense*

1st Squadron, 7th Cavalry Regiment Bradley mechanics install a Bradley power pack—consisting of a General Electric transmission (left) and Cummins diesel engine (right)—at Camp Taji, Iraq, December 2006. *US Army photo by Staff Sgt. Jon Cupp*

Since prior to World War II, Army fighting vehicles have carried a simple star to identify them as American. The stars were often large and bright yellow or white, but when it was realized the enemy used them as aiming points, GIs covered them with mud or painted them out. This tradition of a star to identify a US Army vehicle continues (here on an M3A0 Bradley), although the star is black and small in size. *Photo courtesy US Army Heritage and Education Center, Carlisle Barracks, Pennsylvania*

This handle on an M3A0's left side, behind the driver's hatch, manually activates the Halon fire suppression system from outside the vehicle. Inside the Bradley are sensors that activate in less than a tenth of a second if a fire is detected—in the engine compartment of the M2A2/M3A2 is an extinguisher with 3.2 kg of Halon, while the rear troop compartment's two automatic extinguishers hold 2.3 kg of Halon each. GIs also have two hand-held extinguishers close at hand if needed. *Photo courtesy US Army Heritage and Education Center, Carlisle Barracks, Pennsylvania*

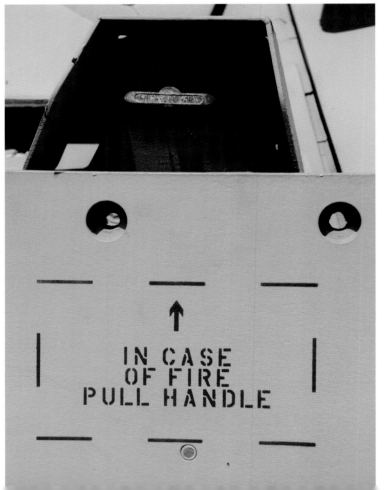

The GI gear strapped to this Bradley's side shows how cluttered AFVs become once outside the motor pool. Black rectangular brush guard hooked onto the left front fender often holds GI water cans. Note attached Multiple Integrated Laser Engagement System (MILES) training gear: the Flash Weapon Effect Signature Simulator (FLASHWESS), clamped to the 25 mm Bushmaster barrel, emits blinking lights to simulate 25 mm gun firing. The orange "whoopee light" or "gumball machine" on the turret rear—much to the crew's annoyance—will flash brightly when the vehicle is "hit." *US Army photo courtesy Department of Defense*

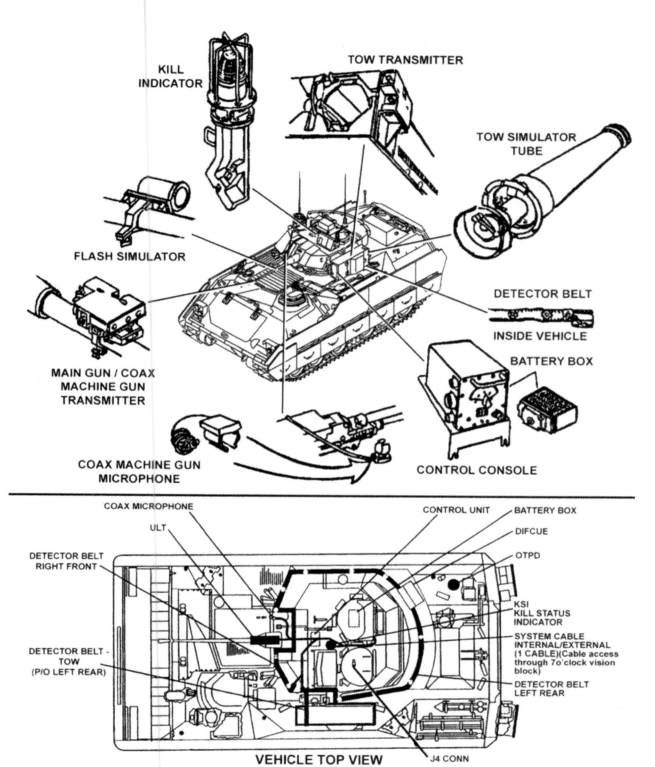

KILL
INDICATOR

TOW TRANSMITTER

TOW SIMULATOR
TUBE

FLASH SIMULATOR

DETECTOR BELT

INSIDE VEHICLE

BATTERY BOX

MAIN GUN / COAX
MACHINE GUN
TRANSMITTER

COAX MACHINE GUN
MICROPHONE

CONTROL CONSOLE

COAX MICROPHONE

CONTROL UNIT

BATTERY BOX

ULT

DIFCUE

DETECTOR BELT
RIGHT FRONT

OTPD

KSI
KILL STATUS
INDICATOR

SYSTEM CABLE
INTERNAL/EXTERNAL
(1 CABLE)(Cable access
through 7o'clock vision
block)

DETECTOR BELT -
TOW
(P/O LEFT REAR)

DETECTOR BELT
LEFT REAR

VEHICLE TOP VIEW

J4 CONN

Components of the
MILES 2000 system,
and vehicle mounting
locations on the
Bradley. *Illustration
courtesy US Army FM
23-1, Bradley Gunnery*

The TOW missile housing on the Bradley's right side contains two missiles, fired one at a time. As this is one of the few flat surfaces free of protrusions like nuts and bolts, this is a convenient location for unique crew vehicle names and/or artwork. Under the tube-shaped engine maintenance platform seen here are brackets for pioneer tools. *Photo courtesy US Army Heritage and Education Center, Carlisle Barracks, Pennsylvania*

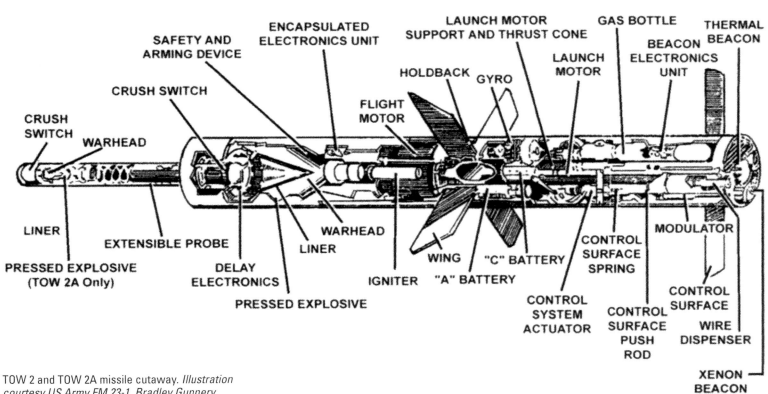

TOW 2 and TOW 2A missile cutaway. *Illustration courtesy US Army FM 23-1, Bradley Gunnery*

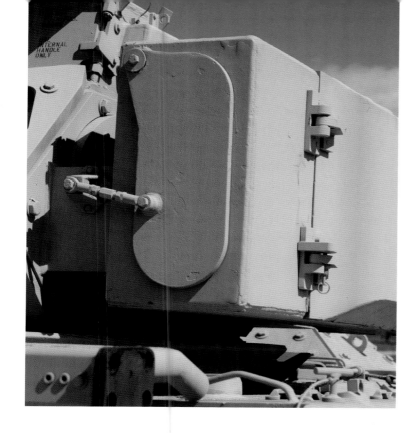

When the TOW launcher is raised to the firing position, gravity swings this oval-shaped cover down and away to allow firing. Not seen here is a canvas dust cover, attached to the rear of the launcher with snap fasteners and hook and loop strips, to protect the TOW launcher tubes from dirt and debris. The large crew compartment on the top rear of the vehicle allows crews to reload the TOW, but only when stopped. *Photo courtesy US Army Heritage and Education Center, Carlisle Barracks, Pennsylvania*

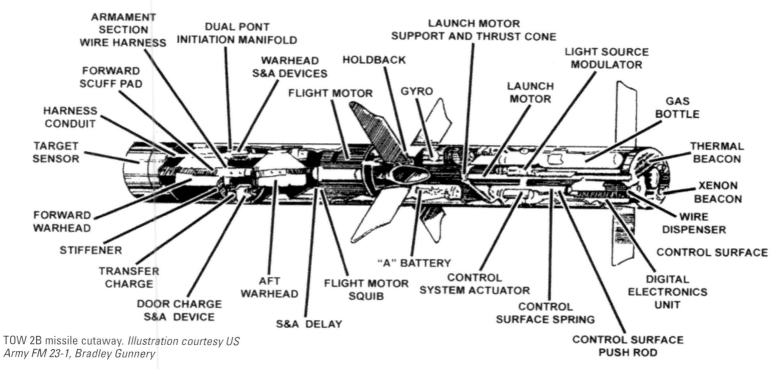

TOW 2B missile cutaway. *Illustration courtesy US Army FM 23-1, Bradley Gunnery*

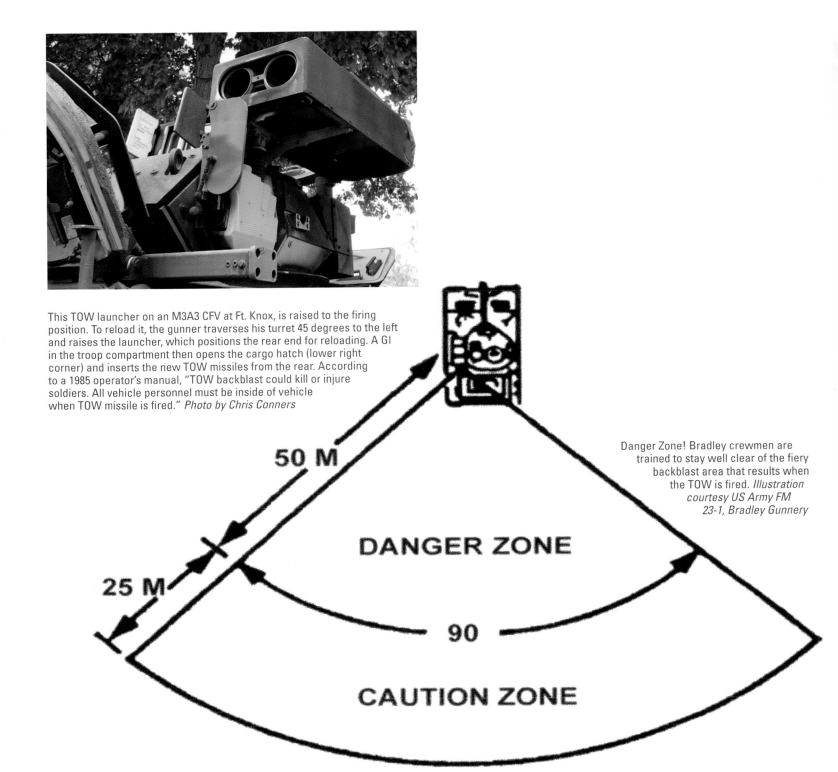

This TOW launcher on an M3A3 CFV at Ft. Knox, is raised to the firing position. To reload it, the gunner traverses his turret 45 degrees to the left and raises the launcher, which positions the rear end for reloading. A GI in the troop compartment then opens the cargo hatch (lower right corner) and inserts the new TOW missiles from the rear. According to a 1985 operator's manual, "TOW backblast could kill or injure soldiers. All vehicle personnel must be inside of vehicle when TOW missile is fired." *Photo by Chris Conners*

Danger Zone! Bradley crewmen are trained to stay well clear of the fiery backblast area that results when the TOW is fired. *Illustration courtesy US Army FM 23-1, Bradley Gunnery*

50 M

25 M

DANGER ZONE

90

CAUTION ZONE

Live fire—Grafenwoehr! In June 2014, 12th Cavalry Regiment, 1st Cavalry Division troopers launch TOW missiles during Operation Joint Resolve, a multinational training exercise. The fiery backblast shows why GIs are taught to keep well clear. The TOW has been steadily improved; with a 3,750-meter range, the TOW 2B can "see" through dust, smoke, fog, and dark, and its hollow-head warhead can penetrate up to 35.5 inches of enemy armor. Note large, waffled Combat Identification Panels (CIPs) on hull sides.
US Army photo by Captain John Farmer

Spreading out large nets like this onto the vehicle, while improving camouflage, is impractical in training because MILES II sensors will not register simulated "hits" if covered up. Bulky nets also hinder the crew from easily reaching gear stored under them. Along with this multicolored net to simulate foliage, Bradleys carry a multi-purpose, solid green or tan tarpaulin, used to shield the crew from rain and sun, or to connect a company commander's vehicle back to back with others, to serve as a company command post or Tactical Operations Center (TOC) in the field. *Photo by Richard Brian*

Looking into the troop compartment of an M2A3. To improve crew survivability, later models of the Bradley include "spall liners" (Kevlar blankets or curtains) in the driver's and troop compartments to absorb fragments and bullets if the vehicle is hit. Ammunition, mine, and flare stowage have also been moved into the hull bottom and rear, to reduce the risk of fire when hit. *Photo by Richard Eshleman*

Because this Bradley crew has raised its 25 mm Bushmaster barrel—SOP while entering or exiting a firing range—it gives us a rare view of the barrel's fluted shape. Later Bradley model coaxial machine guns (to the Bushmaster's left) are "unshrouded" (uncovered). Both weapons are stabilized, able to fire on the move, quite an advantage over many Soviet designs. *US Army photo courtesy Department of Defense*

Night fire! An M2A3 of the 3rd Armored Brigade Combat Team, 1st Cavalry Division participates in Table VI gunnery qualification at the Udairi Range Complex, Camp Buehring, Kuwait, in March 2017. *US Army photo by SSG Leah Kirkpatrick*

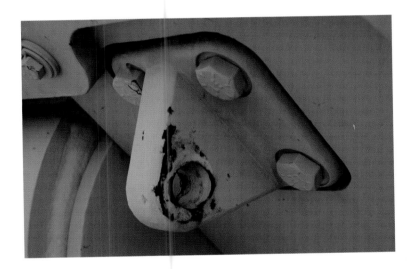

These simple eyelets on the front and rear lower hull allow tow hooks and cables to be attached. *Photo courtesy US Army Heritage and Education Center, Carlisle Barracks, Pennsylvania*

Bradley crews can train safely, economically, and conveniently by using a "Conduct of Fire Trainer," a walk-in, videogame-like simulator that approximates a Bradley's interior. This one is located at the Grafenwoehr Training Area in Bavaria in 2009. *US Army photo by Gertrud Zach*

The deceptively simple finish on this new M2A3 of the Nevada Army National Guard is a feast for model builders, with unpainted natural metal tow hooks, tan paint overspray on the rubber fenders, and the clean, rust-free condition of the tracks. The tall commander's independent thermal vision tower (CITV) that characterizes the M2A3 is prominent on the turret top. *Photo by Keith Rogers*

National Training Center, Ft. Irwin California, February 2015. A Bradley of the 9th Cavalry Regiment, 1st Cavalry Division, with ramp down and troop compartment lights on during Decisive Action Rotation exercise. *US Army photo by Sgt. Richard Jones, Jr.*

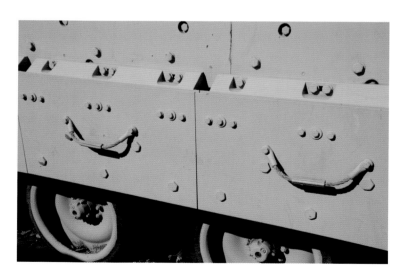

In addition to the larger turret stowage rack, later Bradley variants include wire rope loops like this on the side of the hull, to which soldiers tie or bungee cord a wide variety of gear. *Photo courtesy US Army Heritage and Education Center, Carlisle Barracks, Pennsylvania*

No soldier wants to end a hard training day in inclement weather by sliding into a wet sleeping bag. Holes on the turret's rear bustle rack allow drainage of gear stored there. *Photo courtesy US Army Heritage and Education Center, Carlisle Barracks, Pennsylvania*

Ft. Stewart, Georgia. During a June 2016 Gunnery Skills Test (GST) for soldiers of the 7th Infantry Regiment, 3rd Infantry Division, two GIs install part of a Bushmaster. Notice the height of the Bradleys behind them. *US Army photo by PFC Payton Wilson*

Close-up of the muzzle brake on the 25 mm Bushmaster's fluted, rifled barrel. The M242 is capable of flat trajectory rapid fire against enemy troops in the open, light armor, and low-flying aircraft. It fires ammunition such as the M919 Armor Piercing, Fin Stabilized, Discarding Sabot Tracer (APFSDS-T) and, in training, the M791 Target Practice Discarding Sabot Tracer (TP-DST). *Photo courtesy US Army Heritage and Education Center, Carlisle Barracks, Pennsylvania*

Track maintenance is an important and frequent duty for crews of tracked vehicles, who inspect for proper tension and lubricating oil levels. These soldiers wear the three-color desert combat uniform that replaced the 1980s-era "chocolate chip" pattern, which became a symbol of Desert Shield/Desert Storm. *US Army photo courtesy Department of Defense*

A 3rd Infantry Division sergeant installs a barrel during a Gunnery Skills Test (GST) at Ft. Stewart, June 2016. Interesting details include the mismatched green smoke grenade launchers and the individual track link mounted near the soldier's left foot. The Bushmaster's barrel, unlike those on the Abrams tanks the author crewed, can be quickly removed and replaced as needed. The black rectangle at lower center is a rubber brush guard, used to carry and protect GI water cans, packs, and other gear.
US Army photo by PFC Payton Wilson

Armed and dangerous! At Camp Taji, Iraq, during a morale visit to 4th Infantry Division GIs in March 2008, "Hollywood Ambassador" Gabrielle Tuite displays a belt of 25 mm Bushmaster ammunition. The yellow paint identifies it as a High Explosive (HE) Type M792-T or HEI-T (High Explosive Incendiary-Tracer); Armor-Piercing (AP) rounds have black tips. *US Army photo by Sgt. Zachary Mott*

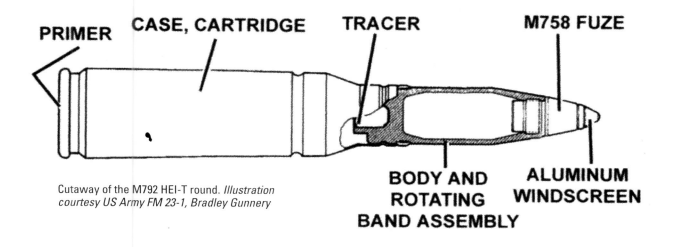

PRIMER

CASE, CARTRIDGE

TRACER

M758 FUZE

BODY AND ROTATING BAND ASSEMBLY

ALUMINUM WINDSCREEN

Cutaway of the M792 HEI-T round. *Illustration courtesy US Army FM 23-1, Bradley Gunnery*

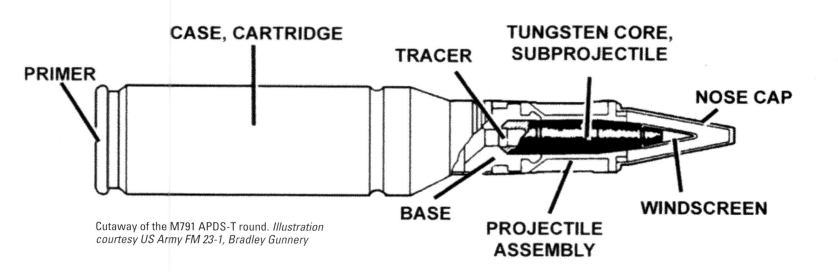

CASE, CARTRIDGE

TRACER

TUNGSTEN CORE, SUBPROJECTILE

PRIMER

NOSE CAP

BASE

PROJECTILE ASSEMBLY

WINDSCREEN

Cutaway of the M791 APDS-T round. *Illustration courtesy US Army FM 23-1, Bradley Gunnery*

Close-up of the "doghouse doors" that protect the gunner and commander's Integrated Sight Unit (ISU), which can see through night, smoke, and haze. When the crew turns the day and night sight cover handles inside the turret, these doors open upwards. *Photo courtesy US Army Heritage and Education Center, Carlisle Barracks, Pennsylvania*

The track commander and the gunner sit side by side in the two-man turret. Here, a 9th Cavalry Regiment, 1st Cavalry Division sergeant inspects controls at Ft. Hood, in October 2014. The vision block (periscope) on left appears to have been removed for inspection and cleaning. *US Army photo by Sgt. Quentin Johnson*

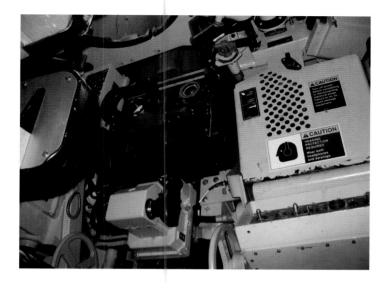

Looking up at an M3A3 CFV gunner's station. Silver rectangle (left) is gunner's seat back. In front of this are his hand controls or "Cadillacs." Above them are the day and night sights, with a rubber face pad for protection during bumpy rides. The black-tipped level to right of the sight opens the "doghouse" doors that protect the sights—up for open, down for close. The gunner uses the thermal-imaging Integrated Sight Unit (ISU) to aim the 25 mm cannon, coaxial machine gun, and TOW launcher. He can flip from 4x vision (low) to 12x (high), and as he lases the target to determine distance, easy-to-read displays tell him the range and type of ammunition indexed and ready to fire.
Photo by Chris Conners

Not to Scale

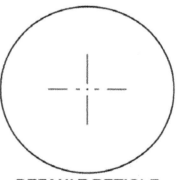

DEFAULT RETICLE

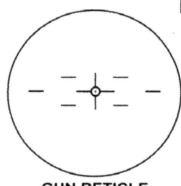

GUN RETICLE

The Bradley gunner can choose from various reticles to sight on his target. *Illustration courtesy US Army FM 23-1, Bradley Gunnery*

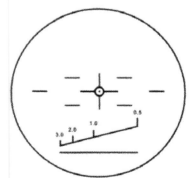

GUN RETICLE WITH STADIA LINES

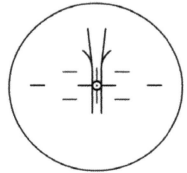

GUN RETICLE WITH AIR DEFENSE RETICLE

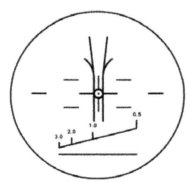

GUN RETICLE WITH STADIA LINES AND AIR DEFENSE RETICLE

This sand-painted Bradley's crew has used foliage to improve its camouflage. With Bradleys being used all around the world, desert-camouflaged vehicles turn up Stateside and in Europe, while Bradleys in European paint schemes have been used in the desert. Note that smoke grenade projectors (lower right) are from a green-painted vehicle—as the author learned as an Abrams tank crewman, parts swapping to keep vehicles operational is common, with little regard for matching colors. *US Army photo courtesy Department of Defense*

Operation Baton Rouge, Samarra, Iraq, September 2004. Seen through a night sight, a Bradley attached to the 1st Battalion of the 4th Cavalry Regiment, 1st Infantry Division, lets loose at the enemy with its 25 mm Bushmaster cannon. *Photo by SSG Shane Cuomo, USAF, courtesy Department of Defense*

Soldiers from the 8th Infantry Regiment out of Ft. Carson, Colorado, patrol the streets of Mosul in April 2008. This photo shows the added ERA armor tiles and boxes to good effect—notice the mismatched color of the tiles. Hollywood and model builders notwithstanding, American armor doesn't always sport precisely matched parts and color schemes. *US Army photo by Sgt. John Crosby*

September 2010. At Camp Beuhring, Kuwait, soldiers prepare their Bradley for Operation New Dawn. Notice eagle artwork on the turret face. *US Army photo*

"Hurry up and wait," Swietozow, Poland. Operation Atlantic Resolve in January 2017, deployed some 2,700 vehicles to Europe. Here, a GI of the 1st Battalion, 68th Armor Regiment, attached to the 4th Infantry Division, takes cover against the snow, and cold. GIs securing their vehicles for the night can cover them with a standard issue 17´ by 12´ nylon tarp, to keep the crew hatches free of rain, snow and ice and avoid delays in moving out the next morning. *US Army photo by Staff Sgt. Timothy Hughes*

A 66th Armor Regiment M2A3 opens up with its M242 chain gun during night fire certification at the Udairi Range, Kuwait, in April 2015. Green and red lights are probably chemical sticks, often used in color combinations for identification and signaling. *US Army photo by Staff Sgt. Grady Jones, courtesy Department of Defense*

Rear turret of an M3A3 CFV, with the commander's CITV rotated down when not in use. To the right, a sturdy guard for the whip radio antenna. The many round bolts on the turret sides enable additional armor to be attached as needed. At lower left, the rear troop hatch used to reload the TOW is in the open position. Notice its desert sand color—since hatch interiors are usually painted to match the vehicle's exterior finish, this indicates that the hatch is a replacement, or the whole vehicle may have been repainted after originally wearing a Desert Sand finish.
Photo by Chris Conners

Samarra, Iraq, September 2004. Like the Abrams tank, the Bradley's thermal sights can see through haze, smoke, and darkness. Because they detect differences in temperature, an enemy armored vehicle's engine appears as white against a green background. Here, a 4th Cavalry Regiment, 1st Infantry Division Bradley fires its 25 mm gun during Operation Baton Rouge. *US Army photo courtesy Department of Defense*

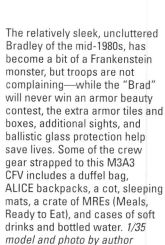

The relatively sleek, uncluttered Bradley of the mid-1980s, has become a bit of a Frankenstein monster, but troops are not complaining—while the "Brad" will never win an armor beauty contest, the extra armor tiles and boxes, additional sights, and ballistic glass protection help save lives. Some of the crew gear strapped to this M3A3 CFV includes a duffel bag, ALICE backpacks, a cot, sleeping mats, a crate of MREs (Meals, Ready to Eat), and cases of soft drinks and bottled water. *1/35 model and photo by author*

Dismount! 5th Cavalry Regiment, 1st Cavalry Division troopers conduct live fire certification training at Grafenwoehr, Germany, in June 2014. *US Army photo by Cpt. John Farmer*

In July 2017, during NATO's Operation Noble Partner, a GI guides a Bradley off a railhead in Vaziani, the Republic of Georgia. While the soldier wears the Army's new Operational Camouflage Pattern (OCP) uniform, which debuted in 2015, the Bradley is painted a solid green color, not unlike the first models of the early 1980s! *US Army photo by PFC Joseph Cannon*

CALFEX, Ft. Stewart. A 64th Armor Regiment M2A2 on the move during Combined Arms Live Fire Exercise (CALFEX) in February 2017. *US Army photo by MAJ Randy Ready*

"Bravo 1-4." While operating north of Tikrit, Iraq, with the 22nd Infantry Regiment, 4th Infantry Division in October 2003, this M2A2 was hit by an antitank mine, killing driver Sgt. James Powell. Returned to the US, it could have been headed for the scrap heap, cut up, or melted down. *Photo courtesy National Infantry Museum*

Instead, LTC Steve Russell, who had led the 1-22 Infantry in Iraq, convinced the Army to donate "Bravo 1-4" to the National Infantry Museum at Ft. Benning, where in 2007, it was lowered into the building, then under construction. *US Army photo by Kristin Molinaro*

"Bravo 1-4" has gone from the battlefield to the scrap heap to become an active memorial to all Bradley crews, seen by thousands of museum visitors yearly. Used in the hunt for Saddam Hussein, today it forms part of the National Museum of Infantry's state-of-the-art "Last Hundred Yards" exhibit.
Photo courtesy National Infantry Museum

Bibliography

Antal, John F. *Armor Attacks: The Tank Platoon*. New York: Presidio, 1991.

Bohm, Walter, and Peter Siebert. *M2A2/M3A2 Bradley: Backbone of the US Mechanized Infantry*, Mini Color Series 7506. Hong Kong: Concord Publications, 2003.

Boly, William. "The $13 Billion Dud." *California Magazine*, February 1983.

Burton, James G. *The Pentagon Wars: Reformers Challenge the Old Guard*. Annapolis, MD: Naval Institute Press, 1993.

Campbell, John T. *Desert War: The New Conflict between the US and Iraq*. New York: New American Library, 2003.

Chadwick, Frank. *Desert Shield Fact Book*. Normal, IL: Game Designers' Workshop, 1991.

Clancy, Tom. *Armored Cav: A Guided Tour of an Armored Cavalry Regiment*. New York: Berkley Books, 1994.

Doyle, David. *M2/M3 Bradley in Action*. (Rev. ed. of 1992 original. Carrollton, TX: Squadron/Signal Publications, 2015.

Green, Michael, and Greg Stewart. *M2/M3 Bradley*. Firepower Pictorials 1010, Second edition. Hong Kong: Concord Publications, 1990.

Guardia, Mike. *The Fires of Babylon: Eagle Troop and the Battle of 73 Easting*. Havertown, PA: Casemate, 2015.

Haworth, W. Blair, Jr. "Moving Target: The U.S. Army Infantry Fighting Vehicle Program in the 1970s." *In Providing the Means of War: Historical Perspectives on Defense Acquisition*. 1945–2000. Edited by Shannon A. Brown, 183–98. Washington, DC: US Army Center of Military History/Industrial College of the Armed Forces, 2005.

Headquarters, Department of the Army. *Field Manual 3-22.1 (FM 23-1) Bradley Gunnery*. Washington, DC: Department of the Army, November 2003.

Headquarters, Department of the Army. *Combat Vehicle Pre-combat Checklist for Fighting Vehicle, Infantry, M2A2 and Fighting Vehicle, Cavalry, M3A2*. Washington, DC: Department of the Army, February 1991.

Headquarters, Department of the Army. *Technical Manual/Operator's Manual for Fighting Vehicle, Infantry, M2A2 ODS and Fighting Vehicle, Cavalry, M3A2 ODS (Hull)*. Washington, DC: Department of the Army, May 2003.

Headquarters, Department of the Army. *Technical Manual/Operator's Manual for Fighting Vehicle, Infantry, M2, and Fighting Vehicle, Cavalry, M3 (Turret)*. Washington, DC: Department of the Army, January 1985.

Hunnicutt, Richard P. *Bradley: A History of American Fighting and Support Vehicles*. Brattleboro, VT: Echo Point Books, 2015.

Macgregor, Douglas. *Warrior's Rage: The Great Tank Battle of 73 Easting*. Annapolis, MD: Naval Institute Press, 2009.

MacPherson, Myra. "The Man Who Made War on a Weapon." *Washington Post*, May 8, 1986.

Mesko, Jim. *M2/M3 Bradley in Action*. Carrollton, Texas: Squadron/Signal Publications, 1992.

Murray, Williamson, and Robert H. Scales Jr. *The Iraq War: A Military History*. Cambridge, MA: Belknap Press of Harvard University Press, 2003.

General Accounting Office. *Operation Desert Storm: Early Performance Assessment of Bradley and Abrams*. Washington, DC: USGAO, 1992.

Verlinden, Francois, Willy Peeters, and Patrick J. Cooney. *M2/M3 Bradley Infantry Fighting Vehicle/Cavalry Fighting Vehicle*. War Machines 5. Lier, Belgium: Verlinden, 1991.

Zucchino, David. *Thunder Run: The Armored Strike to Capture Baghdad*. New York: Atlantic Monthly Books, 2004.

Zwilling, Ralph. *M2A3 Bradley*. Fast Track Series 3. Erlangen, Germany: Tankograd, 2014.